JENNY SMEDLEY

PAST LIFE
ANGELS

T0154681

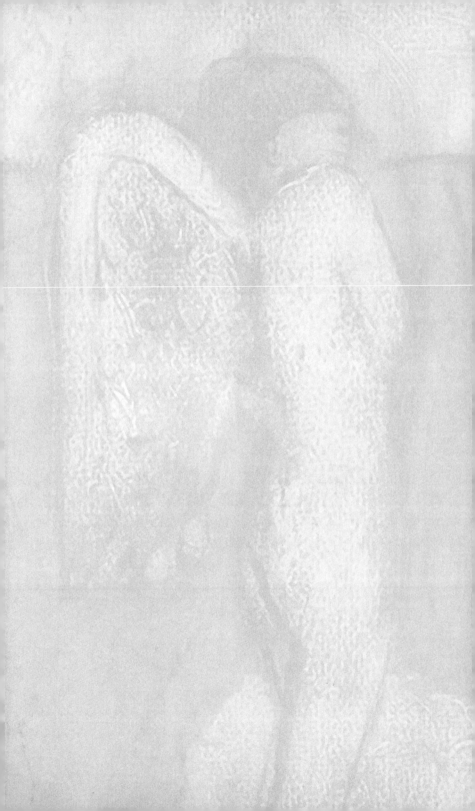

Dedications

This book is dedicated first and foremost
to my husband, Tony.

It is also dedicated to my dog, Ace,
who died in June 2004. She is now back
with us for her third lifetime. We can learn
huge amounts from the developing souls
in animals, if we take the time.

Copyright © 2005 O Books
O Books is an imprint of John Hunt Publishing Ltd., The Bothy,
Deershot Lodge, Park Lane, Ropley, Hants, SO24 0BE, UK
office@johnhunt-publishing.com
www.O-books.net

Distribution in:
UK
Orca Book Services
orders@orcabookservices.co.uk
Tel: 01202 665432 Fax: 01202 666219 Int. code (44)

USA and Canada
NBN
custserv@nbnbooks.com
Tel: 1 800 462 6420 Fax: 1 800 338 4550

Australia
Brumby Books
sales@brumbybooks.com
Tel: 61 3 9761 5535 Fax: 61 3 9761 7095

New Zealand
Peaceful Living
books@peaceful-living.co.nz
Tel: 64 7 57 18105 Fax: 64 7 57 18513

Singapore
STP
davidbuckland@tlp.com.sg
Tel: 65 6276 Fax: 65 6276 7119

South Africa
Alternative Books
altbook@global.co.za
Tel: 27 011 792 7730 Fax: 27 011 972 7787

Text: © 2005 Jenny Smedley
Reprinted 2005
Design: BookDesign™, London, UK

ISBN 1 905047 31 2

A CIP catalogue record for this book is available from the British
Library.

Printed in the USA by Maple-Vail Manufacturing Group

JENNY SMEDLEY

PAST LIFE ANGELS

Discovering your life's master-plan

BOOKS

WINCHESTER UK
NEW YORK USA

Contents

Preface		9
Introduction		10
Chapter 1	What are Angels?	13
Chapter 2	Past Life Angels	21
Chapter 3	Why Past Lives are Important to your Future	33
Chapter 4	Past Life Trauma Symptoms	45
Chapter 5	Classic Carry-overs of Past Life Trauma	53
Chapter 6	Repetitive Behavior Patterns	71
Chapter 7	Phobias etc	87
Chapter 8	Communication with Past Life Angels	105
Chapter 9	Family Circles	117
Chapter 10	Non-Blood Relationships	131
Chapter 11	Why We Live More Than Once	139
Chapter 12	Past Lives and Suicide	151
Chapter 13	Children and Past Lives	161
Chapter 14	Remembering your Master Plan and Sticking to it	173
Appendix:	Therapists	189

Preface

This is a book about Past Life Angels.

These angels spend a lot of their time trying to get through to people in order to remind them what's really going on, and who they really are. One of the reasons for this is that before we're born we have a master plan, a definite goal in this lifetime. It's something we know we have to do, and it can vary from a great lifetime quest, to something as simple as unfinished business that we have to complete. The problem is that once we're born, parents, peers, partners, teachers, and bosses, change us. They don't mean to, but they do.

Our angels are always trying to jog our memories, knock our subconscious into "go" mode, and one of the ways they do this is to nudge us along with past life clues. It may seem like déjà vu, coincidence, or sometimes dreams or obsessions, but the clues are there. If they can kick start our higher self into operation, life changes beyond recognition.

In this book I will share with the reader what I have learned on my journey through interaction with my angels, and show them how they can learn to hear theirs, change their lives to what they were meant to be, and remember **who they really are.**

Introduction

In order to demonstrate how a Past Life Angel can send communication to us, I'd like to share one I got from my own angel. This angel contains, or is united with, the soul of a Native American Indian I once shared a lifetime with, whom I call Jayella. I believe his Earth name was actually Yellow Jay. This message came to me by my using "automatic writing." This means that by using meditation, you can write down a communication because your hand will be guided by the angel. This is what the angel said:

You must learn to see your physical aspect as being a droplet in an ocean. After each lifetime the droplet that contains your earthly experiences falls back into the pool, naturally finding your soul group's place in the whole. From here the things you have learned will dissolve into universal consciousness, thus benefiting the many. The good of the many will be created by the one.

Your soul group will welcome you with arms of light, as if you were an eagle soaring up to its nest on the mountaintop. Here, in the bosom of your spiritual family you will experience the love that you have missed on the earth plane. You will rest in peace.

But, duty will call; your emotional tie to learning from a human perspective will tempt you down from the mountain, and pull you back into the fray. Your soul will pour like quicksilver into a new body and you will begin the journey again.

However, your journey will be different next time, for an

awakened soul has the benefit of memory. No longer will you fear human pain and suffering; no longer will death's shadow overlook you. The sting of death will be plucked, for you will know that the very essence of you is elsewhere, that earthly, human frailty is a mere illusion. The illusion is necessary for those of lower enlightenment, for they could not survive intact, knowing all whilst not understanding.

Men travel through their lives not being aware that the tragedies and sadness they endure are to be swept away on a tide of joy. They do not know that if they could but banish fear and mistrust they would quickly reach fulfillment and their final contribution would be complete. Their journey is full of darkness and uncertainty.

For you, uplifted and empowered child, it will be different. Life in your human shell will be but a simple sojourn, undertaken with delight, and with hunger for experience. You will understand that what you see and feel on this plane is not one hundredth of your whole. Your life on earth is but the tip of the iceberg of your being; the remainder floats above and below, and encompasses all.

As your physical frame was created for you from star material, and as you therefore came to the earth from the stars, so you will return in time. From this day you will know, in the very depths of your soul, that you are a cog in the revolution of evolution. The time is coming when all you have brought to spirit will be utilized to allow your fellow travelers their moment of being lifted to the light. At the right moment, because of your efforts, my child, we will achieve critical mass. All of your fellow men will be awakened at the same moment, and life on the planet will never fear receding into the darkness again. This is all your doing. Be joyful.

You can get this kind of thing too – read on…

CHAPTER 1

what are angels?

What are Angels?

The word angel originated from the Latin *angelus*, itself derived from the Greek word that means "messenger." So, in its simplest term, an angel is an intermediary between man and God, bringing information we need from that God. We need a go-between because God's direct energy would be too powerful for us, so angels act as "transformers," downgrading the energy into something we can cope with. I don't believe in God as a person. To me the concept of God looking like and behaving like a "super" man of some sort, is not viable. I believe that the entire Universe is made up of intelligence, and that "God" is the name for this power. "May the force be with you," is not so far from the truth.

Scientists have recently "discovered" other parallel dimensions to this one, and I believe that "God" exists in the highest, with the angels in the various ones in between. How close we on Earth are to the lowest dimension will be determined by us and our actions in the next few years.

Whatever your picture of God, or what he looks like, is, angels will be there alongside him somewhere. Every religion on the planet has its own version of heavenly host, and every religious text has angels in it. There are various types of angels and they all have different roles:

THE SERAPHIM guide us in relationships and encourage love. They are said to be the closest to God, sitting beside his throne. These beings are said to be made of a light so intense that even other angels cannot look at them. This light is caused by their absorption of God's love from such close quarters.

THE CHERUBIM deal with matters of intelligence and insight. These beings are the next nearest to God, and it is they that were sent to expel man from the Garden of Eden.

THRONES are associated with tranquillity and balance, and as such they are the dispensers of God's judgement; acting with impartiality and humility to bring about the wishes of God.

DOMINATIONS are the go-betweens of the angelic realm. They preside over the upper and lower choirs and allot the tasks of the lower angels. In turn they receive their orders from the higher Cherubim. They are not often witnessed on the Earth plane.

PRINCIPALITIES are involved with the world of humans. They are known as the guardians of nations and direct the activities of the other angels who work on the Earth on a physical level.

POWERS show the lower angels how to conduct themselves. They patrol the boundaries between man and God and are there to guide departed souls to heaven.

VIRTUES are the angels that should be prayed to, to ensure good weather. They are the guardians of nature.

ARCHANGELS are those who communicate directly

with humans, and it's to these that our attention should be turned, for they are the ones who constantly strive so hard to help us; something which we tend to make difficult for them. This group includes the principalities, protectors of nations, the archangels, and the angels who protect humans, or Guardian Angels.

The best known archangels are:

Raphael: the healing angel. Many nurses and doctors say that angels have guided them in their work.

> And now the Lord has sent me to heal thee, for I am the **angel Raphael** one of the seven who stand before the Lord. *Book of Tobias*

Gabriel: appears in Daniel 8:15-26 and 9:21-27. Also appears in Luke 1:11.

> Zechariah was in the sanctuary when an angel of the Lord appeared, standing to the right of the incense altar. Then the angel said, "I am Gabriel! I stand in the very presence of God. It was he who sent me to bring you this good news!"

Uriel: is said to be the angel who accompanies death. He is said to stand beside someone who is about to die, to take them to their transformation. Many psychics have said that when the tragedy of September 11 happened, the skies overhead were thick with angels of light, sent to accompany the departed souls to the afterlife.

Michael: appears as a warrior angel in Daniel 10:13, 21; and 12:1. Also in Romans 8:38, Ephesians 1:21 and Colossians 1:16.

Angels transcend any notion of religion. The first knowledge of angels came in 6000 BC, when the Persian religion, Zoroastrianism, brought them to light. This ancient religion is similar in many ways to Judaism, Christianity, and Islam. This Persian culture brought the concept of angels into Judaism.

Islam speaks of the Milaika, who was able to carry messages to Allah from his people, or vice versa. This angel also protects people against evil forces.

Devas are the Buddhist spiritual/celestial equivalent to angels. They are described as very similar, having bodies that are emanations of light or energy. They are also known protectors. These angels are generally confined to just applauding good deeds done by humans, rather than influencing them.

And of course, all so called "New Age" religions, which are actually based on the most ancient religions of all, receive all their messages and signs from angels or spirit guides.

There are sadly, a myriad of differences between the various religions, some of which cause conflict, but there are two areas in which all religions have common ground – one is that of wanting to help mankind to evolve to co-exist with God, and the other is angels.

There are countless stories about how angels come "down" and help people. I have had such experiences myself. In fact they don't come down from any height, what they do is to "come down" in their vibration. The nearer to "God" a being resides, the higher its vibration. The further away, and the nearer they are to the physical, the lower their vibration, which puts us, as humans, at the bottom of the chain. This is why it's very difficult for us to communicate with the higher angels directly. In order that we can get anywhere near actual contact with even the lower angels, we have to learn to meditate so that we can raise our own vibration, and the angels lower theirs. Hence it's much easier to commune with the lower echelon angels.

EVERYDAY ANGELS

There are, however, two groups of angels within our reach in our everyday existence, sometimes without the aid of meditation, although it does usually require some mental focus. One group is our Guardian Angels, with one allotted to each and every soul on earth. These are the angels that send us signs, which some would describe as "coincidences," but are actually synchronicity at work.

Synchronicity, the work tool of guardian angels, is a word we hear bandied about a lot nowadays, but what does it actually mean? Some people say it means that "there is no such thing as a coincidence, and every incident should be valued and followed as a sign."

In my experience this is pretty much true. My understanding is that if you suddenly bump into an old friend, colleague or business acquaintance you haven't seen for a while, the chances are that it means something. Either they will tell you something you need to know, introduce you to someone you need to meet, or even change your life themselves! If you are about to call an old friend and they call you, listen very closely, because your guardian angel has something he wants to tell you.

Suppose you've had a song in your head all day and your partner walks into the house singing the same song. Have a good look at the lyrics because they may have a message for you. So, what this definition means is that you should pay attention to things that could be dismissed as meaningless coincidences, because there is no such thing, and anything that looks meaningless has been placed there by the mystical power that is synchronicity.

Follow the signs. "What signs?" you might ask. Suppose you're driving down the road thinking about making a new business deal and not sure if it's a good idea or not, and the car in front of you has a number plate that reads BIG 123D. This could be interpreted as "Big …Deal – it's as easy as 1, 2, 3." The thing about synchronistic signs is that they nearly always come in threes, so later in the day you might see a hoarding sign that you never saw before, and it kind of jumps out at you, saying, "Today's the day to take a chance…" Later still you might see a newspaper heading that says, '2000 new businesses forecast this year'. All of these things could just be ignored, but a follower of synchronicity will smile and say thank you, and they'll sign the contract.

It must be very difficult for your angels to organize things to happen for you. Imagine trying to nudge one person onto their right path by making them miss a train, or catch an earlier one, so that they "bump into" someone, without messing up the pathway of everyone else too. It must give them headaches! Don't forget that the person that is "bumped into" has to be placed there too.

Some people will say, why all the cloak and dagger stuff, why not just a big sign, saying, "GO THIS WAY" in letters of fire? Of course that would make nonsense of our whole reason for being here. We're here to learn and grow and to listen to those of a higher vibration and to transcend our physical limitations. Synchronicity isn't here to solve all our problems and make life one long parade from start to finish, it's just meant to point us in the right direction. We're shown the route map, but it's up to us whether we follow it. Synchronicity is the Universe working very hard to arrange things so that signs are placed in front of us. All we have to do is wake up and read them. This is hard to do when you are locked into the 'sleep' that passes all too often for reality in this world we live in.

CHAPTER 2

past life angels

Past Life Angels

Lots of people worry that they are not capable of connecting with their angels. They think they will never learn to meditate deeply enough to raise their own vibrations to that of their angels. Because of this they think they will never understand what they are meant to be doing in life, and will never connect to the angel hierarchy as they see others seemingly doing all the time, and they feel that this makes them lesser people. They really don't have to worry. The group of angels that are most important to our spiritual welfare while we are on Earth, use our own subconscious to communicate with us. Everyone can get their messages any time they want to. The lightest meditative state is all that is required to 'hear' or 'see' the messages from these angels, and they can even talk to us in dreams.

These are our Past Life Angels. It took me quite a long time to realize that there are very special entities around that are specifically charged with our spiritual development. Once I understood this though, it became very obvious that it had to be so. Most people are aware of other angel entities that help us, guard us and act as go-betweens in communication between us and the

Creator. There are angels to guide and comfort people through their death, angels to take prayers to God, angels to help us with relationships and teach us to love, angels that deal with intelligence, and harmony and tranquillity. It seems obvious now though, that there has to also be a special league of beings that are there to concentrate on our individual soul paths.

Everyone on the planet gets nudges from their past lives. It may be in the form of flashes and visions, or déjà vu, dreams, phobias or just strong emotional ties to unexplained memories of places or people. These things cannot be coming simply from the person's own subconscious, because if that were so, then it would mean that their subconscious was fully awake and communicating with them regularly and easily. Patently, this is not so, or all our past life memories would be intact. These nudges are coming from an outside agency – an angelic group.

I call these beings Past Life Angels to distinguish them, because unlike those angels who have been with us during this one, current, lifetime, they have been with us since the creation of our soul – and then through every life ever since. There are a myriad of other angels, and much information on them, but the area of Past Life Angels has been overlooked. The time has come for them to be recognized and utilized, so that we can all develop to our best potential; that applies to both us and these special angels.

I first discovered the existence of Past Life Angels eight years ago, although it's only recently that I have understood what I had discovered. The work these angels do is to guide us through our many lifetimes, helping us to learn the lessons we came here to learn, and trying to ensure that we don't go off track and end up repeating old and ingrained mistakes.

I eventually began to realize exactly what I was meant to understand about the special entities when quite by "chance" I got some extra computer software along with a new printer I'd bought. The software in question was an art program. I'd never been much good with them, but I was driven to start experimenting with this one. I was working mostly just with the colors, when I suddenly realized that there was a "being" or even several of them, emerging in each picture I produced. As I went on they became clearer, and then I slowly realized that if I concentrated on one particular person as I did the picture, a more definite and totally original angel would emerge.

Past Life Angels, in the paintings, come in a variety of colors, like species of exotic butterflies. They are often accompanied by, or are holding, globes of colored light. These globes usually contain the essence of another soul, and will be that of someone you knew in a past life, or, it can be a spark of your own soul.

The position of the globe of light, should the angel have one, relates to one of your chakras – the one that needs your attention. So, if the globe is above its head, your crown chakra needs balancing. If the globe is at the feet, then your base chakra needs attention.

The colors that the angels are dressed in, and the color of their wings, can have different meanings for you too. Their color is what is either reflected by the color of your aura, or it's what you need in your aura.

What are auras? As humans we are creatures of electrical impulses, and like any other electrical device we create an energy field around us. This is an aura. Couple that with the fact that we are also spiritual creatures with souls, and you can see how our auras would be much more complex, effective, and informative than that of your hoover or washing machine! Unlike the auras of machines, our auras change color and vibrancy, depending on our physical and spiritual well-being and to a large extent on our personality traits. Our auras emanate from our chakras. Chakra means "wheel" in Sanskrit, and the body has several spinning energy centers that resemble spinning wheels. These chakras, or energy centers, regulate the flow of energy through our spiritual system. There are seven chakras: the crown, brow (or third eye), throat, heart, solar plexus, center, and root, all creating colors in our energy fields.

Once I understood that I was channeling something different and unique for each person, it made me realize that these were entities of a kind I had never thought about before. They were obviously special, and I was being shown one for everyone. It wasn't exactly a puzzle to be solved, but more as if a mist slowly cleared, and I soon realized that what I was portraying were angelic beings that were related to past lives. The past life connection was obvious, because that is the area I have always been led to concentrate on. I thought back over the nudges I'd been given and realized that they couldn't possibly have come solely from my own mind. There was an outside force at work. It didn't take much from there to realize that we all have this outside force at work on us, and that it had to be an individual entity for each person.

So what are the big differences between Guardian Angels and Past Life Angels? Guardian Angels exude a feeling of security and comfort, and make us feel warm, protected, and loved. When they act it's usually in the form of steering us through our day-to-day lives – trying hard to prevent us from changing what is meant to happen to us by causing us to miss trains or be delayed in some way, so that we avoid an accident, or meet somebody we're meant to meet, etc. They are also the beings we pray to when we need help and protection in times of trouble.

Past Life Angels have a very specific job to do. Their task is to waken our subconscious memories. They can do this, because unlike Guardian Angels, Past Life Angels follow our souls' complete progress through time. The picture they see of our soul is a complete overview of its journey. Unlike Guardian Angels, whose job is to help us manifest our own reality in our physical and mortal lifetimes, Past Life Angels are solely concerned with the progress of our spiritual being.

However, our physical lives can change after connection to them, because opening our memories to the distant past also gives us access to skills we never knew we had.

It makes obvious sense that if we have experienced many positively based past lives as artists, carpenters, writers, composers, healers, mathematicians, historians, cooks, teachers, etc, then once we remember who we are, we will also have recollections of these skills that we have spent lifetimes learning. It also makes vital sense that these skills should be built on, rather than pushed away on the tide of convention. These skills have been collected over possibly hundreds of lives, and totally explain the cases of child prodigies that are recorded. It also says to me that when a child shows special talent in a certain area, for instance woodwork, they should be encouraged to pursue and develop that talent, rather than being made to feel stupid because they are not good at, say, languages. In this way they will surely develop into the most amazing engineers, sculptors, artists, etc, whereas otherwise they might remain just "good."

One of the effects on my persona, which demonstrates how mental clarity can be triggered by past lives, was that I was led to start writing songs, and the lyrics poured out of me. I was once asked by a puzzled singer. "Are you a divorced lady?"

"No," I replied. "I've been happily married for 30 years."

"Then you must have been through some tough relationships?"

"No, I met my husband when I was seventeen."

"Then how do you write so convincingly of broken hearts?"

My belief is that once you access past lives, you can of course write about practically anything convincingly, because most of us will have been through almost every emotional scenario imaginable during our journey through them. This applies equally to all creative writing, and is just one way our skills are enhanced when our soul rejoins us on the physical plane.

Past Life Angels are not committed to fulfilling wishes, giving help in times of need, or solace in times of grief. They see each lifetime as a mere drop in the ocean of our being, each mortal episode as nothing more than a stepping-stone for the progress of the soul. They see the whole of our being, of which the current life is no more than the tip on an iceberg, and it is they, above all others, who have to teach us that there is an ultimate benevolent purpose behind everything we go through, good or, seemingly, bad.

They have to teach us to see every ordeal as a valuable learning experience for the soul, and to understand that the best house, car, holiday, or any material possession, is worth absolutely nothing at the end of our life. In this modern world, where so many, tragically, seem to believe that they could be truly, blissfully happy, if only… if only they could win the lottery, if only they were thinner, if only they were famous, the angels have to show us that the only riches we need to accrue are those of spiritual wealth, for that will determine the next life we will face. They have to show us that being beautiful or famous is not the way to spiritual happiness, which is the only happiness they care about. They have to make us remember that true and lasting happiness is that of the soul, and can only come about when the soul is doing what it needs to do. They do this by trying hard to remind us of our past history. Only then will we remember the master plan for our current physical body, which was constructed to enable our soul to carry out the tasks planned for it to do on Earth, in order that it could grow and progress as quickly as possible. Because of their onerous task, they can sometimes seem very hard taskmasters – they have to be.

Having said all that, when they do succeed in waking us up, the past lives the Angels reveal can also change our current lives literally out of all proportion, even if that is not their main objective.

Past Life Angels are with your soul when it transits from life to death. They guide it into the "other" world of spirit, and take care of it while it recovers from, and assimilates data from, the life you just left. They nurse the soul through any healing that needs to take place, and accompany it through regaining divine knowledge. They help the soul to analyze everything that has happened to it through all the lives it has thus far experienced, and advise the soul of what should happen in the next physical life in order that it will develop as it's meant to.

Your angel will then accompany the soul as it's born into its next lifetime, which can be a day, a year, or several hundred years in the future, depending on how much recovery is needed. This next lifetime scale will also depend on other factors, such as whether the soul needs to get back into the physical in time to interact with somebody or with some situation. When we remember who we really are we can also look back over all our lifetimes, not at all confused by the multiple relationships we have had, languages we have spoken, and lifestyles we have led. For we will be just one step from the divine knowledge we have when we are in spirit.

It's also very possible that when the Past Life Angels succeed in their ultimate goal, that of getting us to realize that we have had many lives, and the purpose behind those many lives, it may be a kind of "passing out" for them too. Their future development may depend on ours. It would make sense to me, because I believe that all souls and spirits must progress, to make their existence have meaning, so perhaps Past Life Angels are able to move up, closer to their Creator. This means that we help them in the same way they help us.

When we arrive at the point in a lifetime where we do

remember everything, and start going back over our previous lives, tying up loose ends, finishing unfinished business, righting wrongs, and discovering our true purpose, my belief is that after our death it will not be necessary for us to come back again to this human form. At that point I believe we progress to some sort of higher level.

This should be a comfort to people who tell me they are afraid to look into the subject of their distant past because they can't face the prospect of coming back as someone else. It's actually to their benefit to look into it, because by doing so they might avoid that necessity. Of course, at that point our Past Life Angels will also be free to move on.

People might ask why we need celestial help, and don't just remember everything for ourselves. As the soul is moved into the physical it retains all its knowledge, for a while. The reasons our consciousness forgets are manifold, and start when we are quite young.

First of all it would be too complicated for one physical brain to consciously remember all its previous lives, relationships, language, behavior patterns, etc. Second, one of the points of us being here *is* to remember it all, <u>despite</u> the constraints and distractions of the emotional and physical sensations we go through as humans. Third, we are here to learn by those experiences, and if we knew that was what we were doing, there would be no learning and no opportunity to meld our own body and soul back into one perfect unit…

However, your Past Life Angel's job is to try and bring your subconscious memories to the forefront so that you succeed, because without those little nudges, I don't suppose many of us would ever overcome the huge burden that being physical and emotional puts on us. As life moves on and we are influenced by others and by circumstances, the odds are very much against our becoming whole again without some help. We get more and more deluged by worldly factors, and our memories get more and more submerged beneath material values. We push our impending death out of our minds, because we fear it. And yet logically, if we didn't, we would see that material wealth is so transitory and trivial, and means nothing at all in the end. A spiritual pathway is the only one that makes any sense at all.

Obviously, once a person re-experiences their past life and, most importantly, their past death, they are able to look back on that death. Doing this enables them to see that death is not real, and is only the shedding of physical imperfection, so the fear is removed.

So, we have a hard task in this physical world. We come here with all the knowledge and memories we need securely locked up in our subconscious. They are driven underground by the pressures of fitting into society, earning a living, finding a place and people we can feel secure in and with, squeezing ourselves into whatever box we are made to feel suits us, and our role in the class and social systems of the world. Our task then is to allow our spirit to rise up through all that, to let it supersede all the problems we are faced with, and to bring mind, body, and spirit back together again, after it has been pulled apart by the circumstances of being human. It's no wonder then that the Universe saw reason to provide us with spiritual guides, in the form of our Past Life Angels. Their job is the hardest of all.

why past lives are important to your future

Why Past Lives are Important to your Future

Why do we need to remember our past lives? One all-consuming collective reason for us to all wake up, is for the salvation of every person on the planet, and mankind as a species. It's very easy in this modern, convenience- and industrial-driven world to feel separated from your spirituality, Mother Nature, and the very fabric of our planet. I feel that we need to take a step back and remember that we are linked to every other creature and life form on Earth, and that their fate affects ours too. This isn't always easy to do. Finding a pathway which suits our character and also satisfies the need we all seem to carry deep down in our souls for fulfillment, is difficult.

Many believe, quite wrongly, that 2012 (Ascension) means the end of all who are not spiritually attuned. This is a date referred to in the ancient Mayan calendar, when many people believe the world as we know it will end. It's said that those who have not "raised their vibration" by making immense progress towards spiritual completion, will be doomed, leaving enlightened souls to ascend to some other place, presumably heaven, or its equivalent.

This is not true. What we actually need to know is that by 2012 enough souls must be awake to achieve critical mass, and then everybody will be switched on at once, whether they were awakened before or not. So it's up to each and every individual to play their part, however small, in ensuring the progression of our whole race, by shining our light for all to see.

I can't put a figure on how many souls need to be aware in order to achieve worldwide critical mass. All I do know is that I was angelically defined as a seed planter, by the being that visited me on the train. At the time I had little idea of what that really meant, but now I do. I am a tiny cog in the machine, as we all are, and my role is to plant a seed of awareness in as many people as possible. Every tiny cog is of vital importance to the awareness of the whole. This is simply awareness that what we see with our light-defined vision is not all there is, and that our physical bodies are nothing more than the tip of the iceberg when it comes to our whole selves.

Religion in isolation doesn't really help. It was not invented by one or any combination of the myriad of gods and goddesses, old and new, that people have worshipped over the centuries since man appeared on the face of the planet. Religion was invented by man.

The world in general has drifted so far away from the old beliefs that revered and protected, and worked *with* natural forces, rather than against them, that it is almost impossible for the average person to get in touch with their sixth sense, their intuition. If we could do that, then maybe we could turn back the pages of history and undo some of the damage we have done to this unique and wonderful globe. We have to remember that we and the animals and plants and even rocks that surround us are all part of the same energy system, and that as such we are all in this together. Universal light, or God if you will, is with us at all times and if we could just stop for a moment and reach out to it, we might just be able to save this wonderful and precious planet of which we are caretakers.

We can have the best of everything in a material sense, the best house, holidays, cars, furniture, and yet on the day we die these things will mean absolutely nothing. Spiritual wealth is the only thing that our God, whomever or whatever we assume him to be, will be interested in. Material possessions will mean nothing at all to him.

What people do is to rush through their lives at breakneck speed, not feeling important unless they fit the mould, that is to say, collect what everyone else considers important. They believe that if they could only reach their latest goal, say to get that new three-piece suite before guests arrive for Christmas, then they will achieve that elusive something they have always needed to make them happy. They go through their entire lives this way, always thinking that the next thing will bring them something to fill the void they feel inside. They honestly believe, because they have been brainwashed to, mostly by clever advertising, that something as mundane as a piece of furniture can drive away the darkness that clutches at their heart in the night.

Looking logically, you can easily see how ridiculous that belief really is. What those people don't realize is that the chasm within them is their soul calling out for nourishment and recognition. They run ever faster along the treadmill, and never know that it's themselves they are running from. Because they are going so fast, and never let their minds rest and wander in the tranquil reaches of silence, they miss all the signs their angels are sending, and usually end up sad and embittered, that they never quite reached that elusive goal that would have made them happy. Once people understand this fact they can start to build their real life, their spiritual one. In order to do that, they need to understand how the system works.

When a soul is first created it is a pale colorless thing. It has no depth and is very basic in its awareness. This has to change, as the whole purpose of creating a soul is to create a wondrous spiritual being with depth and energy and power. Obviously, while the Creator can create whatever it wishes with the energy of the Universe, there are limitations. The being we are destined to be requires experiences, emotional warmth and depth, and compassion. These things cannot be taught, they only come from knowledge. So, we need to become human in order to learn these things. It would be no use, however, just throwing our newly formed soul into a human body, because it would not be capable of dealing with everything the human goes through.

So we don't begin as humans. Our soul is divided into thousands, even millions, of scraps, and each of these tiny portions is placed first in inanimate life-forms, such as rocks. From there we progress through plant life, each scrap being carefully collected after its allotted time by our Past Life Angel, and brought back to its collective. Gradually the pieces of soul are colored by experience and gain enough depth to become animal. The beginnings will be very humble, like grasshoppers, tadpoles, and beetles. We will never have any memory of this, because at the time our soul would have been too fragmented.

Again our souls are carefully shepherded by our angel, through the lower animals, until eventually we are placed, maybe in just two parts by now, into a sentient being – perhaps a dog or cat or horse. Finally we are able to become the "engine" for a human body, to do with as we will, and learn as we can.

Once you understand this, you can see very clearly how we are all related, planet, rocks, plants, animals, and humans, and how our destiny in intertwined. This is why cruelty, especially deliberate, to animals is an abomination to the Universe. Empathy is probably the most important emotional response in the Universe, for it is only by feeling what another feels that we can see why cruelty is an abomination in the world.

I've had a couple of wonderful examples of the way that animals not only reincarnate, but also come back several times to the same owner – one whom they know has helped them in the past and will help them again. My own dog has been with me twice already, and has just returned for the third time. The first time she was a small black terrier type dog, called Snoopy. The second time she was a black Labrador cross, called Ace. Ace died in June 2004. When she died she was scarred from an operation to remove a tumor. This meant that one of her teats was missing, and another displaced. We recently found her again – or rather, she found us. She is again a cross Labrador, and again a black bitch. This puppy was born with one teat missing and another which doesn't match up with its partner.

This dog, Kachina (we chose the name because it means 'a doll containing an animal spirit') already knew the house, the garden, and various words of command. Ace's favorite game was to play hide and seek with one of her toys. Kachina knew this game right away, and without any training; at three months of age she was able to seek and find any toy selected at random.

I also got a wonderful story from Margaret. She wrote, "We already had three cats, and although our dear cat, Jed, had died two years ago, we had no intention of getting another cat. Our daughter had taken a friend to choose a kitten. They called to show him to us. But when they tried to leave with him, he clutched me and cried like a baby. The more they tried the more he clung. In the end we just had to keep him. We called him Puska. At ten weeks old Puska knew how to work the cat flap, watched the TV like Jed did, and even stood up like a meerkat to wash, just like Jed used to do. The other cats took no notice of a stranger in their midst, and accepted him as if they already knew him."

Both these are examples of animals almost ready to become human.

Newly "promoted" souls are easy to recognize in their human form. They will be lightweight, have no spiritual depth to them, and be only concerned with the material aspects of life. They can appear dull, but we should nurture them all the same, because they are like children, and need to be taught and have the opportunity to grow within themselves. All the while, as we then progress through at least eighty-five lives, and often well into the hundreds, our angels try and guide and protect us, rejoicing at every tiny move we make towards wholeness, and giving us whatever nudges we allow. As we become more spiritually attuned, obviously our angels are able to communicate more and more to us, until we have advanced far enough to remember who we are.

When I first found out about my own past lives, although it changed my life completely, I was still wary of sounding dogmatic. I used to say that there were many pathways and that everyone must find and walk their own. I still would not try and push anyone to follow my route, but I have vastly increased my belief that past life memory is vital to spiritual progression. This is partly due to making the acquaintance of Past Life Angels, because they wouldn't exist if the subject wasn't so important, but also because the idea of it being so vital follows a powerful chain of logic.

I have people say to me that they have enough problems in this life without worrying about things that happened in the past. There is, of course, the normal answer to this, which is that your past problems are often the cause of your present ones, but it goes a lot deeper than that. Imagine if, in your forties or fifties you were suddenly struck down with total amnesia of everything that had gone before – your family, your loves and hates, your beliefs and experiences. Imagine how it would affect your personality and entire way of life. Imagine how incomplete you would feel, and how you would be desperate to understand yourself. Would you say to me then, "I don't need to remember my past, because I have enough problems with my future?" I don't think so. You would understand that any future progress you might make in life was dependent on who you really were, because anything else would be an illusion that would eventually become unsatisfactory, and you would be desperate to remember. Well, it's the same thing – if you don't have any memory of your whole self and all that has gone into your current make-up then it's like having amnesia of the soul.

There are spiritual reasons, but also physical reasons why you need to remember. In a practical sense, understanding where you came from can radically alter your current circumstances. When I had my experience ten years ago, which enabled me to remember my past life, albeit in a rather brutal fashion, all I could see was that it gave me peace after some 400 years of grief. A lifelong depression was ended by the revelations, and for some time that was miracle enough, but the changes were like a set of dominos toppling over, and they are still falling. Once the gates are open, the river of self-knowledge runs free, and as you learn more about yourself, you find that you can do more than you ever dreamed possible.

Remembering past lives is the trigger that enables you to remember the whole of your being, mind, body, and spirit, and to reunite the three. This, and learning the lessons we need to advance our soul, is the purpose of coming to this world.

When we come to this world as babies, our memories are all intact, but as almost everybody discovers, these memories soon fade away. This is due to our trying to fit into our allotted space in society. When we are first born we are made to feel elite. We see our parents as some sort of benevolent giants, and we rely on them for everything. With kind parents, a baby is always told it is good and beautiful, no matter what it does, and even passing "giants" stop to utter words of admiration about it. Not surprising then that it comes as a terrible shock when suddenly one day, these giants, who up till then have done nothing but lavish love and praise on us, suddenly turn on us with harsh words, and from that moment we will do anything to remove that perceived threat. Wanting us to fit into society, our parents start to change us, by chastising us when our behavior doesn't meet their criteria of acceptable. Because at that age our parents are gods to us, we want and feel a desperate need to please them, feeling that our very survival depends on it.

This in itself isn't the problem. We all have to learn to live among others in harmony, if we're to survive. The problem is that in our attempt to fit in we quash individuality out of ourselves, and this in turn pushes our spirituality into the background, sometimes extinguishing it altogether for the sake of conformity. What happens gradually then, over our formative years, is that we become almost completely contained in our physical body and we become focussed on its well-being to the detriment of our souls.

However, it can be said that this is a necessary thing, and that if we can turn the tide and bring our souls back to the forefront, thereby reuniting body, mind, and soul, we will have achieved what we set out to do. We need to do this because by re-consolidating our whole in this way, we enhance and multiply the energy that is the core of our being and existence, making us progress up the ladder towards our ultimate goal. What this goal is will remain unknown until we reach it. So, we need to achieve this reunion in each life that we live, in order that we become "educated," "well-rounded," and "balanced" spiritual entities, worthy of and deep enough for advancement.

Most of us follow the norm. We are indoctrinated to think,

"I must conform." It starts when we are small. We have to learn to fit into the home and family. This is of course necessary, but the process is sudden and traumatic, from loved and beautified infant to naughty child who must learn a lot of rules in order to be loved – or that's how it feels. Then we go to school and our peers soon teach us that there is a new set of rules there, and if we don't learn and obey them, we will be left out or bullied. Teachers tell us that if we don't learn certain things by rote, we will be losers. We might have a strong penchant for something rather more creative than academic, but instead of that small talent being nurtured, it's pushed aside and we are packed full of information that we are probably not suited to ever use.

This is very sad because sometimes being channeled into the mainstream of learning, means that skills inherited from our vast experience in other lives are turned aside, and we are forced, instead of nurturing them, to struggle with subjects we are not best equipped to absorb.

Then the workplace looms, and a sex life. During this most confusing time we find ourselves thinking, "I'm at a certain age, I must earn enough to make a life," "I'm at a certain age, I must find a partner," "I'm at a certain age, I must buy a house, have children, etc." Before long the leap is made to, "I must have the best house," "I must have a new kitchen," etc and there we are, immersed in the physical and material. Our spirits have drowned in it and, sadly, a huge number of people wait until they are in their forties or fifties before they seriously consider the most important part of themselves – their soul. I am no exception to that. All through these times our Past Life Angel is walking alongside us, desperately trying to reach our inner selves. It wasn't until I was forty-five that my Past Life Angel managed to get through to me.

past life trauma symptoms

Past Life Trauma Symptoms

People ask how they are to know if there is a past life they need to remember. One should assume that this is so, because our past incarnations hold the key to progress in our spiritual development. Experience has taught me that without exception people have an inbuilt need to know who they are and what they are here for. They have a need to know a purpose for their lives, and you can't find out where you are going until you know where you have been.

This need can be compared with those of an adopted child. These children almost always have a desperate need to know the facts about their biological parents, even if they play no part whatsoever in their lives. They feel that they will never understand themselves unless they can first understand and know their real parents.

However, having said all that, there are symptoms that tell you that you have past lives that need immediate attention, as well as nudges from your Past Life Angels.

One of the most validating things I have discovered from all the letters I receive from readers of my past life column in *Chat*

It's Fate magazine, is that most people are looking for the answer to the same question – why am I here? Some try and do it logically and scientifically, but most are looking for a mystical reason for their being. The majority of letters I get are from people suffering either depression or phobias and panic attacks, for which they can find no reason, and these are all symptoms of past life traumas. The people suffering from depression are desperately searching for an elusive *something* that they can't define, a reason for being. They believe that there is *something* vital that they should be doing, but can't find it.

These people are rushing through their lives looking for something to fill the void they feel inside. Some say they feel they are not really living, just acting out a role. They appear alright on the surface, but are sinking like a stone inside. They feel cut off and alone, even within a group of people. That's because the loneliness they feel is not that of a person seeking company, it is the loneliness of their body seeking a union with their soul. They often say that they feel detached, as if they are out of place. Of course they are also out of time, because they are still attached to their own past and not really living in the moment, in its truest sense.

People often end up in a pit of despair, saying that they need somebody to throw them a lifeline. They feel hollow inside and yet there, within, is the very place where their soul is waiting to give them everything they need.

It's a classic symptom of body, mind, and soul drifting apart, when people find themselves knowing that they are missing something but are unable to classify it or reach for it. I was the same. At the height of my depression I cast about for that elusive *something,* turning from project to project, as I failed to grasp what it could be that would bring me satisfaction.

I read this time after time in letters, "Why do I have such bad luck?" "Why am I so miserable?" "Why does God keep me here, when my life is so useless?" It's very sad and it makes me want to shout from the rooftops, "Find out who you are!"

I also get letters from people who cannot understand why relationships have gone sour, or who ask why they have obsessions with certain periods, strange emotional attachments (or feelings of not belonging) to people or places, frightening nightmares, links to places they have never seen, or mental problems that lead to self-harm.

Anorexia, for example, is a symptom of something that went badly wrong in the past and has left a scar on the soul that needs to be cleared before it will stop affecting the current lifetime. Therapist Julie Winstanley gave me a great example of how this can work. Her client was an anorexic who had tried everything to understand her problem. Finally she listened to her angels, and a spark of her soul must have been ready to understand, because she went to Julie to be regressed. It turned out that she had been locked in a dark room in a past life, being fed by a man who visited her daily. She never knew anything else apart from the room, and the fact that she was totally dependent on the man and couldn't feed herself. Then the man stopped coming and she died of starvation. This led to her having a new understanding of her "problem," and allowed her to move on positively, addressing her weight concerns sensibly, without blame. Of course this will also open her up to further memories and therefore spiritual development. Conversely, if she hadn't found the cause of her health issue, it would have got much more serious instead of being alleviated.

These stories demonstrate that once we co-operate with our angels, we will be healed. Mind, body, and spirit will be gradually healed of emotional and physical trauma that is brought about by remnants of the past.

I get letters from people who are suffering ill health and they ask, "What did I do in a past life that I should be punished like this?" Of course the answer is "nothing," because it's not a question of punishment. Ill health is yet another symptom of the past. These things are yet more nudges to try and wake us up spiritually. You can understand why such drastic measures are taken if you can grasp just how *important* this awakening is. The nudge is possible because we develop a problem that relates to our past. For instance, if someone was beheaded in a past life, then they might develop neck problems. If they were killed at age forty-five in their previous life, then at the same age this time they will get symptoms associated with it. The vital thing is that if they understand why they have the neck problem and bring their attention to what their Past Life Angel is showing them, the pain will not develop but fade instead. If not, then the problem will worsen into something more serious.

Unexplained pains that doctors cannot find a cause for can also be past life manifestations. I had such a pain that turned out to be where, not I, but my past life husband was stabbed. It faded away as soon as I realized what it was, even though I'd had it for over forty years on and off.

Stabbing can also cause weight gain. It makes sense that

someone thin is in much greater danger of a fatal injury from a knife or sword than a fat person, the latter having layers of flesh protecting their vital organs. So, somebody who was stabbed might be unintentionally over-eating in order to build up a layer of protection. I also had this problem "sympathetically," like the pain. Again, once I had realized why, the weight disappeared with the pain.

Today, one in fifty people in the USA suffer from OCD – Obsessive Compulsive Disorder. It can consist of things such as hours of hand washing, special rituals that need to be undertaken before the person can leave the house, or driving round the block over and over again, convinced that you need to keep checking for accidents. These are just a few examples of this distressing illness. These people have a need to perform these acts to try and calm their minds and make them feel that "everything is alright." Of course this can be a symptom of a past life. Obsessive cleanliness for instance can be a hang-over compulsion from having lived in the time of plague. This can also cause a fear of vomiting. Being convinced that you are about to witness a road accident can, of course, be because at one time, which you have forgotten, you did.

Another common plea I get in my letters is from people asking why they feel like a man in a woman's body, or vice versa. When you think about it, transsexuals go to the most extraordinary lengths to redress what they see as a mistake of birth. They take social steps, such as cross-dressing, which can make them outcasts among their friends, and even among their families. They will accept financial ruin, and even mutilating surgery, all to make themselves feel real and comfortable in their own bodies. This kind of compulsion is extraordinary when you think about it.

One possible explanation for this is that the person may have spent ninety-nine out of a hundred lives as a man, perhaps, for instance, as a military officer, and not be able to adapt when they suddenly find themselves as a woman, expected to keep house and bear children. Imagine a person who has spent lives in female bodies, dressed in crinolines, corsets, and silk negligees, only to suddenly find themselves in a man's body, and expected to work on a building site as a laborer. No wonder confusion over roles can set in!

When it comes to homosexuals — there are a plethora of psychological, physiological, and emotional explanations why a woman would prefer a sexual relationship with another woman, or a man with a man. However, leaving these aside, I believe that there could be a past life connection here too. It's very possible, when someone has always had man/woman preferences, and yet suddenly appears to switch most unexpectedly at some point in their life, that they have suddenly met a person of the same sex who was their partner in a previous life. To this person the sex of their partner will be quite immaterial really, and they will be drawn to the other soul, whatever the circumstances.

These letters demonstrate the vital reason most people have for remembering who they really *are*, by remembering who they really *were*. Most of my readers' misery or bemusement is caused by the fact that they subconsciously remember a past life that is struggling to come to the surface.

It's also because before they came to this lifetime they had a master plan. It could be something quite mundane, such as finding someone they knew in a previous life, or righting a wrong they committed against someone else in another life. It can be that there was something they knew they would be in a position to achieve, but whatever it was, they have forgotten it at the same time as they allowed their soul to become detached from their mind and body. This frustration nags and rankles at them, and they often become sour and disillusioned, just waiting for life to pass them by, or even ending it prematurely because they can't stand it any longer.

If you are able to reconnect with your soul, then you become a complete entity, but one thing you need to do to make that happen is to remember your previous lives. Why? Because your past is the vital element you feel is missing from your soul. Recapture it and your soul becomes complete. When that happens there isn't anything you can't do.

classic carry-overs of past life trauma

Classic Carry-overs of Past Life Trauma

GUILT

A symptom of a past that desperately needs to be brought through to the present is that of unexplained guilt. We often carry through feelings of being guilty for acts that took place in our distant past. This is not a good thing because it interferes with our current learning, and also because it makes no sense.

We are not the people of our past; the subtle difference is that we have *evolved* from that person. We can't continue to carry round packages of guilt that arose from learning opportunities both for us and for our perceived victim.

CASE ONE

The signs and nudges that Sandy Miller was getting were damaging her life. She knew that there was something wrong with her self-perception of always being a victim, and yet conventional thinking could not resolve the problem. This is often how it works, and it demonstrates that, sadly, our past lives, which we have to learn to take as a priority, are often almost the last thing we consider when it comes to problem-solving. It turned out that Sandy was suffering from carry-over guilt, and this was making her "want" to be a victim to atone for what she did in the past. She had to first understand why she felt the way she did, and then learn to forgive her old self, so that she could progress.

Sandy went to see Sunny Satin, a very experienced regression therapist, who practices in Los Angeles and New Delhi. The memories that came through for Sandy were amazing, and one can see how life after life has been blighted, as her angel has tried desperately to get through to her time and time again. Sandy has been going round and round in circles, because like many people she became hopelessly confused. So she was a victim, not only of guilt, but also of "repetitive behavior." Finally, this time around, in this life, communication was established, and she was "triggered" into seeking the right help.

Sunny took Sandy into a deep trance. Her first response to the question of her surroundings was that she could only see darkness. Despite finally "getting there," it was obvious that Sandy's mind was still blocking the answers she needed. This is more proof that outside agencies are prompting us into action, because otherwise Sandy's subconscious would have been more co-operative. Sunny was able, with persistence, to open Sandy to the past. She finally reached the first relevant lifetime.

He did this by instructing her to look for the origin of her problem and go back there.

Sandy saw herself as a man in a desert. He was about thirty years of age and was standing outside his home, a hut. There were several children playing nearby, and "Sandy" was their father.

"Sandy" told Sunny that there had been no rain. All the animals had died and there was no food or water. "Sandy" explained that he had been the owner of a herd of goats, but that during the dry time many of the goats had died, and the others had been killed to feed the children. Now the seven children, including babies, were all starving and dying of thirst. He said that they cried all the time. The well had dried up too, and "Sandy" decided that he had to go and try to find some food and water somewhere for his family.

He seemed very distressed that the children were always crying, and yet a little irritated by the constant noise too. The complaints, including those from his wife, were getting on "Sandy's" nerves. He also felt very helpless and decided that he had to leave, both to relieve himself of the wailing and to try and find help.

After a long walk he ended up at the nearest town. He thought he might be able to get some work and use that to buy food to take back to his family. There was a working well in the town, so he'd take water too once he had some food. He managed to get some work stacking goods for an old man and got paid some money. There was enough money to buy grain but, before he went to buy it, "Sandy" decided that he had also earned a drink after working hard. He was tempted into a tavern, spending some of the vital money on alcohol. The situation was bad, but still redeemable, but then he met a woman.

"Sandy" rebelled. He felt that his whole life had no

pleasure in it, so he decided to stay with the woman. He ate, drank, and soon forgot about his family waiting for him back home. He gave the rest of his money to the woman in exchange for spending the night with her in her room in the tavern. The next day he couldn't go home empty-handed, so he had to find another day's work. Sadly, the previous day repeated itself, and he found himself once more, drunk and almost penniless. The same woman persuaded him that it was too dark for him to set off home, so "Sandy" stayed the night again. He woke in the morning to discover that the woman had taken the rest of his money.

The next day "Sandy" only managed to find enough work to earn a loaf of bread, but he decided to go home anyway with the little he had. He drew a bucket of water from the well and set off. It was hot and took a long time. Some of the water spilled and some evaporated, but there was still a little in the bucket when he reached his home.

The place was deserted, and his family where nowhere to be found. He walked around, checked the neighbors, and then finally found his wife and children huddled together in the desert. Some of the children had died, and the rest, with his wife, were crying in misery. His wife and children wouldn't even look at him. When he told his wife he'd managed to get a little food and water, she told him, "You're too late."

"Sandy" threw himself down on his babies' graves and wept. He stayed there all night, and in the morning his wife came out and said to him, "What's done is done. It's time to come home."

"Sandy" knew he didn't deserve to be forgiven and knew that his wife could only do it because she, and the children, still needed him. All the bread and water he'd brought back was gone. They decided that they had to leave their home and go to his wife's family. The wife's father had a big house with livestock, and "Sandy" hoped to get work there. "Sandy" spent the rest of that life ashamed because he had let his family down and also ashamed because he had failed to be the "man" of the family. His wife's family were angry at him for letting his pride stand in the way of bringing the children to them for help sooner.

Later, Sandy remembered her name in that life. It was Mahatma. Mahatma's wife was Ravi, and by the time of this memory, they were both around thirty years old. Mahatma was at the grave of his children who had died as a result of him wasting his money on drink and a woman. When Ravi's father had found out about it all, he had made Mahatma leave. Ravi and the children stayed with her father, so Mahatma was all alone. He was living in the family's mud hut and feeling ashamed and miserable. He decided that he couldn't live with his pain and so was not bothering to look for food or water for himself; he just spent all his days at the grave of his children. It got harder and harder for him to walk out to the graves. Finally he died, all alone, lying on the graves.

Sunny instructed Sandy to look down at Mahatma's body and asked her to tell him what lessons had been learned from that lifetime. Sandy said, "That your family are the most important people to you. It's not always about having a good time. I lost everything because of what I did."

Sunny discovered by questioning Sandy that she had been suffering the guilt and shame of that lifetime for seven other lives, including the one she was currently living. Sunny knew that in order to get away from this destructive repetitive behavior, Sandy had to disassociate herself from Mahatma and also forgive him. It wasn't easy, as this guilt had been festering for hundreds of years but, finally, Sunny heard the words he needed to hear from Sandy.

She said, "I can forgive him as long as he doesn't ever do it again. I forgive myself... and make a vow to myself to never get distracted from my children's needs again for my own purposes, for my own entertainment or enjoyment."

Sunny instructed her, "All right, now when I count to three, you're going to forget about him completely. Now just come back to this room and forget about everything you've seen and experienced and with each and every breath just get more and more relaxed and comfortable with yourself. As of today, your life is taking a new direction. And the misery that you have suffered in the last seven lifetimes is going to stop."

Sandy should be congratulated for allowing herself to finally open up and stop the punishment she had been going through. The guilt she felt was making her virtually instruct her own subconscious to make her into a victim, because that's what she felt she deserved to be, after her behavior as Mahatma. The subconscious is like a computer. It never forgets what is put inside it, and it's very difficult to re-program it, once it has been instructed to fulfil destructive predictions. That should be rectified now and Sandy will find that her life starts to blossom. She will, of course, still get nudges, but now the door is open a little bit, it will get easier for her to wake up to all of her real possibilities.

CASE TWO

This second case was reported to me by Brenda White of Nottinghamshire:

> John was a client in his forties who received hypnotherapy for help with a number of issues, one of which was a feeling of guilt that he could just not shake off. He presumed it was due to an affair he had with a married woman when he was just a teenager. We tackled all the other issues first and lastly came to the guilt. During the session he reported he felt he was flying through space and time. I immediately realized this could be a spontaneous regression so I reassured him and went with it.
>
> "I'm travelling through space, very fast... I'm going through time...
> I'm up in the sky looking down... I see a woman in a crowd... she's looking up at me... she looks familiar, oh, she's my wife... my present wife...
>
> "I see a man in a monk's gown on his knees looking up with his arms stretched out upwards... he's desperately praying to God for forgiveness. He's in a church... there's fire all around him... everything is burning... all the people are dead...
>
> "He's a priest... It's me... I'm the priest... There's another man ... authority, he's caused the burning, to stop the people fighting back. Tyranny... Christianity... Catholics... Protestants... I'm Catholic,

authority is Protestant.

"He burnt down my church! I couldn't stop the people being killed, there were so many attackers! I was the priest and I had an affair with the woman. I am the one who committed the sin and she is the one who is punished...

"I am responsible for their deaths... I told them they would be safe in the church... they believed me... I now have to die."

So he was a priest who told his followers that he would protect them and that they would be safe in the church. As all the people were killed except him, he was racked with guilt and killed himself by making no attempt to escape the fire because felt he deserved to die.

I explained to him that there was no need for this guilt to continue because he had killed himself in self-punishment and so his debt had already been paid, adding there was no way he could have saved them because they were grossly outnumbered. I also told him that because he had prayed for forgiveness before he died, he had repented his sins. Also, as the woman with whom he had an affair is his present wife, it could be viewed that his sins have been forgiven as he is now being allowed to love this woman again, this time within the sanctity of marriage. After my explanation, he accepted that he can now let go of the guilt. Notice I only focus on resolving the guilt and do not search for historical information.

After I brought him round it took him a while to

compose himself and then he gave me some more details. He told me that it happened in Spain around 400 years ago. He then told me that from being a child he had always wanted to be a priest but his parents had talked him out of it, also he is the only one in his family with olive colored skin and does have a Spanish look about him. He said he had not believed in past lives before this session and was completely taken aback by this event. He said, "It's answered so many questions, and it was so real, I was actually there."

So he was partially right when he first told me he felt the guilt was linked with an affair, but it was not from when he was a teenager in this life, but an affair he had 400 years ago!_

INABILITY TO DEAL WITH PROBLEMS

There are people who seem to be incapable of dealing with life's twists and turns, and when this happens they have a tendency to run away in some form or another. This can be manifested as not being able to commit to a relationship, family, or career, or as moving house or area every time things get difficult, thinking that a change of scene will cure things. This does sometimes work, for a while, but inevitably the problems will resurface and ask to be faced again. Angels have a hard time getting through to people like this, because they and their nudges are also seen as problems to be run away from. In the case of Jasmine, her method of running away was extraordinary. She would have an accident that resulted in amnesia and so, effectively, the problem was gone. Not only was this disruptive, it was also dangerous to her health and so she came to realize that she had to take some action to confront it. She lived in Thailand, so she went to regressionist Katharina Bless.

In the regression, Jasmine found herself on a beautiful tropical island beach, with coconut trees, white sand, and a brilliant blue ocean. There were also cliffs and a grotto, and the sand was dotted with shells and white pebbles. There was a small path leading up to what Jasmine felt was a village. Jasmine was middle-aged and had long hair that she could feel blowing in the wind as she stood and looked at the ocean.

Katharina instructed Jasmine to walk along the path towards the village. She then entered an area of jungle-like growth, and eventually approached a group of huts. They were simple wooden houses, built in a circle with a fire area in the center. Inside the huts, Jasmine found pots with food and water in them. She told Katharina that the place felt untouched by time, secluded and cut off from the world, which she believed was experiencing the mid 1800s. Jasmine came across the people who lived in the village, and realized that she didn't know them.

Abruptly, Jasmine left that time and found herself somewhere else, in Central America. She was in another village, this time that of some Indians. She could see people putting fish out in the sun to dry and stripping some reeds to make baskets with. Jasmine felt that she was a teacher of the children, but that it was not the place of her birth. On answering Katharina's questions, Jasmine revealed that she had arrived there from the sea, coming ashore amid big waves that threatened to drown her. It turned out that Jasmine had arrived in a boat, but she was injured. She had neck and head wounds when the people of the village dragged her ailing boat onto the safety of the beach.

This was just a start for Jasmine, who would need more sessions to totally uncover the causes of her problems, but she had this to say: "Ever since the session I've had a conscious thought process throughout my daily activities of a desire to face the fears and pains. I intend for this to become clearer."

INABILITY TO SUSTAIN RELATIONSHIPS

This is another classic symptom of past life dysfunction. I have two very good examples of this. The first is with Sally. She was having doubts about her relationship. She never felt really able to commit to a man and still feel secure. She went to see therapist Julie Winstanley, and this is what they discovered together.

Sally remembered being in a cathedral, and she could see the pipes of a very big church organ. She was wearing a long cotton dress in gray or mauve, and a coat and bonnet. There was a big wooden door and Julie instructed her to go through it. This brought her into the main body of the cathedral, where there were big pillars and wooden pews. It was cold in there. Sally wasn't able to remember her own name.

The year was somewhere in the 1800s. Sally was a teacher in that life, a governess, and she lived with the family whose children she looked after. She felt very frustrated with her life because she knew she could have achieved a lot more if she'd had the chance. She told Julie that this had proved impossible because she wasn't of the right class. Sally had been brought up in an orphanage, and she couldn't remember her natural family, or what had happened to them. The orphanage was run by nuns, and Sally could remember their black habits. She said the nuns were strict but kind, and that she had a special friend called Maggie.

Julie discovered that Sally was waiting in the cathedral for someone. It was a man, someone from the family she worked for, but he didn't come. Sally believed she was in love with this man, Henry, but she admitted that he was very unreliable. She described him as, "aged twenty-nine; tall and handsome, dark, long sideburns, very smart, wears a top hat." Henry was the brother of the mistress of the house where Sally worked as a governess. Their relationship was a secret, because if she was found out, Sally would be sacked.

Later in the regression Sally revealed that she had ended her days living alone in Manchester. She was sixty-three when she died. She never married and of course Henry never committed himself to her. But Sally learned a very important thing that was to change her current life. As she died back in the 1800s, she realized that she had been loved. Her children – her pupils – had all loved her very much. The love she'd desperately needed came not from a man after all.

It seems to me that "Sally" was unable to commit in this lifetime for two reasons. First, because she felt the commitment would not be reciprocated and, second, because she found in her past life that the love/satisfaction/appreciation she sought was more forthcoming from her career than from a man.

Once she understood this she would have started to have

a new perception of herself. The woman she was obviously gained great satisfaction from the love her pupils showed her, and this will have increased Sally's self-esteem and belief in herself. It will also have showed her that the reasons that she can't commit are not the fault of her prospective partner in this life, but left-over doubts from her time with "Henry." As a result of this she will be able to move on and allow him to commit to her, and she to him, without fear. She will also know that love of and from a partner is not necessary to find fulfillment, because in her past life she DID find fulfillment from her career, and this comfort will allow her to let love thrive naturally in this life.

She will, of course, also have awakened parts of her subconscious that were dormant and been able to glimpse her true and entire self. Her Past Life Angel has made a start on her transformation.

Some people feel that they are definitely with the right person, but still there is some kind of a barrier to them having complete trust in each other. Paula was one such person. I sent her to Janet Thompson to see if the doubts she was getting were messages from her Past Life Angel, pushing her to uncover past lives.

Paula was in a new relationship with Robert, and wanted to know where and when they had been together before. Paula wanted to know about lives when she had known her partner Robert, because emotionally she was finding it really hard to trust him, and was finding it hard to believe all the wonderful things he said about her. Janet took Paula to four lives in which she had known Robert before. In two they were happily married; in one she was forced to marry another; and the other one is as follows.

She was taken back through this life with the breathing technique, letting go of any negative feelings and emotions, back to her early childhood and back into the womb. Then she was asked to bring her feelings and emotions for Robert back into her body and consciousness and then allow those feelings to take her back in time and space back into that other life when she and Robert were together.

Paula saw a kitchen. It looked medieval to her, and "Robert" was there too, looking much as he does today, and she knew that he was her husband in that life. He was fifteen years older than his wife. Paula was wearing long robes with a headdress that covered her hair. She had a belt or rope around her waist. She was in the kitchen preparing vegetables for a meal. When questioned, Paula told Julie that she and the man had been married for a long time, but had no children. There had been a miscarriage, which affected both of them badly.

Paula described the house they lived in: "There's a heavy wooden door that opens up into another room, there's another fire place, a very large fireplace. It feels quite damp and there are candles, quite a lot of candles. There's a funny smell, quite an acrid smell. There's a staircase, so there's an upstairs. The walls are a very, very thick stone and there is one bedroom upstairs and a straw mattress; it feels lovely in there."

It was a peaceful and fairly uneventful life. It was described by Paula as "rhythmical," as it followed the seasons. "Robert" died first and Paula followed him. So, there was one lifetime where "Robert" and she had been in love and their life had been reasonably content.

The next life that Paula re-visited was not so happy. At the age of fourteen she was living in Rome, the servant girl to her employer, Robert, whose name was Marcus in that lifetime. Marcus was married to a cruel woman, who treated the servants badly. Marcus was often away from home, leaving his servants, including "Paula" to abuse from the lady of the house. Much though she disliked the wife, Paula liked the husband very much. She said, "He pulls my hair when she's not looking."

One balmy night Marcus came across "Paula" in the garden. He touched her shoulder, pulled her hair gently, and turned her around to face him. Inevitably, he kissed her. The servant girl was excited by the kiss and welcomed it, but suddenly, Marcus pushed her away, because his wife had come into the garden. The wife must have been suspicious because she wanted to know what "Paula" was doing out there, and when she was told, she didn't seem to believe the girl.

Marcus and "Paula" became lovers, and it seemed that the wife knew about it, but chose to keep quiet. The wife became very ill after giving birth to a baby, and was confined to her bed most of the time. "Paula" loved Marcus very much and by the time she was twenty, she was totally devoted to him, believing that he loved her too. When Marcus' wife died, "Paula" said she tried to be sad, but deep down she couldn't help but be happy, for surely he would marry her now.

It didn't work out that way. Marcus was given promotion in the army, and was moved away. The household was split up, and "Paula" found herself being relocated and sold to another household in Florence. She was heartbroken. Marcus told her that he still loved her, but that he was going to do his duty. "Paula's" new mistress was kind enough to her, but at the age of twenty-one, without Marcus, she felt that her life was over. She was freer in Florence and able to go to some social occasions, but she didn't warm to any of the young men she met. The spark had gone out of her life and she was lonely, as she was the only servant.

There was a fire at the house and "Paula" was killed. She had tried to escape the flames and smoke, but something fell on her head and knocked her unconscious. Julie went through a healing process on Paula, and then they moved onto the next life, which Julie felt might be important.

It was in 1742. Paula knew her own name this time. It was Louise. She was sixteen years old and in a drawing room, having tea with two army officers. The two men were rivals for Louise's affections. Louise preferred the dark-haired one, whose name was Jonathon, but he was unsuitable to marry as he was not wealthy enough to please Louise's rich family. They lived in a large house in Lincolnshire and Louise had a pony that she rode in the grounds. The other man was called Mathew, and the two men had come from London for the weekend to see Louise. They were all excited about the ball that was going to be held in the house.

During the ball Louise's parents encouraged her to dance with Mathew, who was considered suitable marriage material, but Louise wanted to dance with Jonathon, who was being very persistent. In the end she agreed to dance with him. He told her that he was in love with her, and she left the ballroom with him to take some air. It was a beautiful night and Louise was very flirtatious with Jonathon, even though she knew it was wrong to lead him on. Finally, Jonathon kissed her, and much though she didn't want to, Louise enjoyed it. But her father saw them and was furious.

Louise continued to flirt with Jonathon on every possible occasion, and told him that she loved him too, even though it wasn't really true, and could come to nothing. He became very distressed when she refused his marriage proposal, then he got angry at the way she had encouraged him, and had promised him things she would never be able to deliver.

Louise's father had arranged a marriage for her and she felt she had no option but to comply with his wishes, although it hurt her to let Jonathon down. She married her father's choice – a man called Michael, who was a "good match" and very wealthy. He was much older than her, being thirty years old to her eighteen, and she found him very dull. When Louise fell pregnant to Michael she succumbed to a difficult birth and died. She was relieved she said, "to leave."

Paula's reaction to her memories was this: "Knowing that Robert and I had been together so many times before, I felt that this time we have come together to really experience the depth of a love that's as old as time. That evening we had the most wonderful romantic time, and when I touched him he said he knew how much I loved him, because he could feel it coming out of me. He was quite emotional about that. Since then I've felt really calm and happy to let things just gently unfold as I know they will."

CHAPTER 6

repetitive behavior cycles

Repetitive Behavior Cycles

Most of the people who read this book will already be in some way enlightened. They will be looking for deeper information to realize the truth of what they already suspect, that there are many layers to a soul. These people will have experienced at least fifty lifetimes, because if it were anything less they probably wouldn't even have picked up this book, or any other on spirituality. This being the case, it becomes obvious that the way to remember their entire being is to remember their other lives.

One area that Past Life Angels have to help us in, is what I call the "carousel" syndrome, or repetitive behavior cycles. Left to our own devices we would quite often get ourselves stuck on a cosmic carousel, reliving scenarios we have experienced before. We would make contracts, while in spirit, with the others involved in the scenarios that "next time" we'll "get it right," only to fail once again, to make the same mistakes again, and to complete yet another life without learning enough from it. This still happens even with Past Life Angels to remind us, so without them it would be hopeless. Once we open ourselves to the divine guidance that

Past Life Angels give us, we remember our previous lives and we can start to tie those loose ends and right those wrongs, because we will remember what happened and with whom.

A classic example of this happening was the case of Gerald and Sophie. They came to me with problems that seemed insurmountable. They both complained that the other treated them little better than a servant, ordering them about and making life a misery. Luckily their angel led them to make contact and ask about their problem, rather than go through another life like that. You can imagine the Past Life Angels discussing this problem, and debating how best to nudge them off of the merry-go-round they were on. After using my Past Life CD together we unearthed a fascinating story. It seemed that life after life they had been repeating their relationship problems. Because they used it together, wrote down what they saw, and then compared notes, I was able to prove to both of them that what they remembered was real, because they both saw the same things.

In one, Gerald was the master and Sophie the servant, in the next it was the other way round. They had also swapped genders several times, presumably in the hope that it would alter things for them. I'm sure that when they were both in spirit they discussed the problem too, and kept on having the very best of intentions of getting it right next time. Of course it had never happened, because what was also carried through, as well as those good intentions, was the resentment of the put-upon party.

In each life they had started out quite well, but sooner or later the old pattern had established itself and off they would go again, breeding more bitterness and resentment each time, until the feelings were so high that *this* time around they had gone for the husband and wife option, hoping that would change things. The only thing that had changed was that they were on an equal footing, but the pain was still there and so all that happened was that they were both domineering and aggressive with each other.

Once they had remembered the past they were able to look to the future with new hope, curb their tongues and emotions, and begin to see each other in a completely new light. They understood that there was no right or wrong as far as they were concerned, and absolutely no point in laying blame, because at one point or another they had both been to blame. The only way forward for them as a couple was if they drew a line under the past and accepted each other without reservation. They had to learn to empathize with each other too.

This can apply to any relationship problem. The root cause of everything from infidelity to domination to lack of confidence to jealousy, irresponsibility, etc, can possibly lie in past lives and the way we have interacted with our partner in them.

Another was the case of Lynn and Paul. When they met they felt they knew each other. Their marriage was expected to be one that was made in heaven. They were soul mates, they were sure of it. Four years and two children later, Paul started to hit Lynn and abuse her in other ways. She was heartbroken and couldn't understand what had happened. Three years and another child later, Lynn had finally had enough and she left with the children. Two years after that Paul still couldn't let go. He didn't really seem to care about the children, but made them the excuse to keep turning up.

Lynn was baffled and she had many questions for me. Why did their marriage go wrong, when they were so sure they were meant for each other? Why did Paul become abusive, when he had seemed so trustworthy at the start? Why wouldn't he leave them alone, now that the break had come? Why couldn't he get on with his own life and let her try and get on with hers?

The answers start with the fact that when they thought they were meant to be together, they were wrong. This often happens. People who knew each other in the past are fooled by the falsely comforting sense of familiarity they get when they meet. They feel they recognize each other, so, therefore, they must be soul mates. No, they recognize each other, but it's just as easy to recognize an old enemy as an old friend. They mistake familiarity and the comfort it brings, in a world where everyone is desperately searching for something and someone to be with, for love. They both appear trustworthy to the other one. Familiarity does that. Look at TV celebrities, for instance. Members of the public don't know them at all, and yet they tend to trust them and feel they are friends — just because they are familiar. The same thing had happened with Lynn and Paul.

Paul became abusive because he grew to feel the old animosity he had felt for Lynn in a previous life. He felt trapped with an enemy, but did not know where the feeling came from. He was almost afraid of Lynn, felt she had power over him, and tried to take it back by using his physical advantage over her.

The reason Paul couldn't leave Lynn alone after the break-up was because he was still troubled by a sense of unfinished business. They had been put here and drawn together in order to put right a wrong, but they hadn't done it, because they didn't remember it, and were in danger of getting into the 'carousel syndrome.'

After joint regression they came to know that in a past life Paul had been a woman, and Lynn a man. Lynn had been responsible for Paul's death. They were drawn together because they did recognize each other. But they had been enemies before, not friends. This was why Paul felt threatened by her in this life even though he was now physically the stronger of the two. Lynn had been a smuggler in the past and the gang had been afraid that "Paul," would betray them, so "she," was murdered.

Once the couple understood why everything had happened, they certainly did not want to be together, but they both had knowledge that helped them come to terms with the past and recover from it. Following my advice they held a ceremony in which they officially forgave each other for the past and thereby released themselves from it. They went their separate ways and made new lives for themselves.

Both these couples had become "stuck." It must be very frustrating for our Past Life Angels to watch us making the same old mistakes over and over, while they frantically try and get our attention.

Most people can relate to a situation where they have felt instantly drawn or repelled by a stranger, or someone they only just met. This can sometimes be explained by their auras being incompatible, but why would this be the case? It is because they subconsciously recognized the person from a past life association. Past Life Angels will sometimes go to extraordinary lengths to bring us face to face with such a person. If you ever feel this way then there is a reason for it. There is no such thing as a meaningless coincidence. If someone you feel strongly about, whether they give you a good or a bad feeling, is thrust into your face, there is a reason for it.

Most likely they will be involved in one of these loose ends that you have come here with the intention of tying up. Most people who have this happen shy away from the encounter because their subconscious knows that they have "been there before," and they don't understand that their angels know that running away from the repeat scenario brings the parties no closer to resolving the issue, or learning from it.

A further example of carousel syndrome is provided by the following regression, reported to me by Brenda White:

Crystal told me that the husband of a friend of hers really gave her the creeps and she always felt very uneasy in his presence. There was no reason for her to feel that way, because he had never done anything untoward to her in this life. This was seriously affecting her relationship with her friend because she was avoiding her so that she would not have to face her husband. Crystal was worried that her friend might be thinking she'd done something to offend her. So she wanted to see if she had known the husband in a previous life.

"It's night time, Plymouth 1756. A big fire in a field, there's the man! He's got a top hat on, just walking up and down. He's got a stick with a gold knob on the end. He's in charge of the colored people, slaves... he's poking them with the stick.

"I'm only a little boy; I'm sat on the floor with a shawl round me, and I'm clinging to my mother. Some other men there are sorting the colored people out, putting them into different groups. We're all going to be split up. Come here on a big boat. This man's gonna sell us. Young children get put with the older women.

"I still see my mother, she works at the big house, Brackenstone, no Branstone. I'm three years old. He's there at the big house. He's evil. He came to the little wooden house and mother has been whipped, Grandma is bathing her sores. Somebody's made a doll, some sort of witchcraft. See him on a black horse, he rides through us and knocks things over. Very evil man... Mother kills herself, she can't take anymore.

"I'm six now. Got burns on my hand, there was a pot hanging from a frame of wood over a fire and he kicked it so the liquid went on my hand, my skin's peeling off, can't take anymore!

"I'm Joshua, I'm ten now, don't think I've got my hand. Have to work in the fields. Just miserable Soams ('the man')... I've gone all cold. It's freezing; can't get warm, there's no wood for the fire. It's freezing.

"I'm thirty-five now, I've got some sort of fever, sweating, but I'm freezing cold. I dig a hole and fill it with straw, that's where I'll be put. Just waiting now for me to die... See bluebells... a wood..."

After the death I asked for her to review that life

and see what lessons there were to learn and she came out with this statement: "From the path, thou shalt take us, something that we believe in… they call it witchcraft. We know the true meaning… Keep the faith regardless."

After this session Crystal reported that she no longer felt uneasy in her friend's husband's presence. She felt calm and had no negative feelings towards him at all.

Another repetitive problem, which just grows and grows through lifetimes, is lack of self-respect and/or self-esteem. If you experience a lifetime of abuse, where you were unable or unwilling to break away, you develop a feeling of helplessness and hopelessness. Then, in your new life, you might feel that there's "no point in trying," that whatever you do won't work, or that someone with power will destroy your dreams. In this way you become a self-fulfilling prophecy, and find yourself enduring yet another lifetime of abuse, which sends your self-esteem spiraling down ever further.

One such person was "Dan." He went to therapist Georgina Cannon to ask whether his serious self-doubts were past-life related. It never fails to amaze me how our angels not only trigger this idea in us, but also make sure we end up with exactly the right person to help us.

This is Georgina's account of the session:

Dan, a blond, blue-eyed, good-looking young man, came into the clinic office hoping to boost his self-esteem. He told me that he had been shy for as long as he could remember, and found it difficult to talk to strangers. He had just moved to Toronto from a small blue-collar northern mining town, and wanted to make living in the city a comfortable experience for himself. He wanted to get past his shyness, so that he would be able to make new friends, and find a good job. We agreed that we could start by using hypnosis to overcome his shyness, and the rest would follow from there.

Dan went into hypnosis easily, and when I asked him to go back to the very first time he felt the shyness, he shifted in the seat, his voice became a whisper, and he shrank back into the chair as if he felt very humbled and self-effacing. He had slipped straight into a past lifetime. He told me that he was a Japanese housewife in the sixteenth century, who was sold to a tyrannical merchant, to become his wife.

"Her" feet were bound – as was the custom then – and because she was a naturally large-boned woman, she was in perpetual pain from the bindings. Her husband beat her regularly and she was frightened to speak to or be seen by him. She spent her life desperately trying to make herself invisible, and was happy to die as an escape from the misery that was her daily life.

As the soul left the body, we both sent compassion to this poor Japanese woman, and forgiveness at all three levels to the husband. Only when this was complete, did we make sure the shyness had left body, mind, and spirit. Joyfully, Dan reported that it had.

On returning to full awareness, Dan excitedly told me that even as a very young child growing up in a 100% white, blue-collar town, he had always been fascinated by Japanese costume and language. So much so, the first thing he did was to find someone, who had since become his friend in Toronto – his only friend at that time, who could teach him Japanese. The language came very easily to him and he was well on his way to becoming fluent after only a couple of months.

Dan told me, "When I moved to Toronto from Sault Ste Marie, I began to take private Japanese lessons and picked the language up very quickly. So much so that when I spoke to Japanese people they would often compliment me on how good my Japanese was and would ask me how long I lived in Japan. I'll never forget some of the surprised looks that I received when I told them that I had never even been to Japan before! I have always had an interest in Japan. From playing Japanese games and watching Japanese cartoons as a child to eating the sushi that I love today, I have always had a deep-rooted interest in things Japanese. When I began exploring my past lives through hypnosis, during one of my sessions I looked down and saw that my feet were bound. Going up my body revealed that I was a Japanese woman in a very elaborate kimono. The images were very clear. And I could actually see and smell everything."

After this session, Dan became a different person, almost overnight, and although he tried to explain the process to his friends and family in his hometown, no one really "bought it" But *he* does… and is living proof of the power of past life regression. ❖

Here's another example of how poor self-image and lack of confidence can stem from the past. This one is also from Georgina Cannon.

Eight years ago, Jim was one of my first clients in the clinic, and he came in for hypnosis treatment for low self-esteem.

It started with a phone call. Jim said, "Hi, I'm an actor, and I can't seem to make even the simplest auditions, because I don't believe I look good enough. In fact, I hate the way I look. Can you help me?"

Of course, I said I couldn't be sure until we had met and I had spent more time with him to find out more about his background and the issue.

That morning I was busy with clients, and when the receptionist buzzed and said Jim was in the reception area, I energetically cleansed the treatment room and centered myself before going out to meet him.

In the waiting room was a tall, well-built (it was summer and he was wearing a tight T-shirt and jeans), very good-looking young man.

He stood up as I came into the reception area, put out his hand and said "Hi, I'm Jim."

His appearance and manner didn't fit at all with the problem he had presented over the telephone, and as we walked toward the treatment room he told me that how he looked on the outside totally belied how he looked on the inside. When we were seated in my consulting room, I asked him to explain himself further.

"I can't explain it," he said, "but I feel so much like an outsider. Like I don't belong anywhere, and when I look at myself in the mirror I feel and see myself as really ugly. My friends think I'm nuts, but that's how I feel, and it is interfering with my acting career. I have a hard time going to auditions, particularly if they are for a romantic lead."

We discussed and agreed to start to work around the issue of self-esteem and then work on audition nerves. Because Jim had been meditating and doing yoga for many years, it was easy for him to slip into hypnosis and regress back to his childhood. While in hypnosis, we discovered that even as a young boy, Jim had felt like he hadn't belonged anywhere, always feeling like an outsider. He had a close relationship with his father, but that was about all. So I facilitated him back even further, into the womb of his mother and beyond.

He suddenly found himself in an oriental palace as a young princess, wearing flowing filmy robes. "She" was about eight years old, living a luxurious life as the only child of the caliph (a regional royal somewhere in the Middle East – maybe Morocco) in about the fourteenth or fifteenth century.

As she laughed and played with the servant's children, the princess had no contact with the outside world at all. On her tenth birthday, her father, the caliph, came to visit her in her area of the castle, bringing with him some of his advisors. They told her that it was time for her to be married and that they would be sending out invitations to the neighboring regions for appropriate arrangements to be considered.

Months went by, and very few young men came to visit. They left shortly after meeting with her. Three years later, with still no promise of marriage, she was ashamed and realized that she had disgraced her father – although she didn't know why. She begged her father to tell her what was happening, and each time he just turned away.

After a while she no longer saw him and spent most of her time alone with the servants. When she was fourteen, she asked her oldest servant to tell her the truth about why she was alone. At first the servant refused, fearing she would be killed or beaten, but eventually seeing her mistress's sadness, she told her the truth. The caliph's daughter had been so protected she hadn't realized that she limped and that her face was half covered with a brown birthmark – and in general she was not pleasing to the eye. She was ugly and unattractive to any suitors looking for a bride.

She became more of a recluse and spent the rest

of her short life living alone in a corner of the castle, disgraced, denounced by her family, unloved, and unwanted by anyone. She died gladly, wanting to leave that rejection behind. However, she had brought it into her current life, by continuously rejecting herself/himself.

I led Jim through an extensive forgiveness program, and he emerged from the hypnosis treatment smiling and laughing and crying! So much time wasted! So much to look forward to! Last time I heard from Jim, he sent me a poster advertising his role as the lead in *Carousel*!

From these sessions the two young men will not only have regained their self-esteem, but many other things, if you think about it. They will both see women in a different light for one thing, and never forget that they are people with the same feelings as men. They will also understand what it's like to be helpless, and under someone else's power, and this will imbue them with great empathy for their fellow creatures. This will ensure that they will never abuse the power that their new lives will surely bestow upon them, now that they have awakened.

It also explains Dan's obsession with all things Japanese, and will thereby alter his perception of that race to include some of the less attractive traditions that go with it. Jim will understand that beauty truly *is* only skin deep, and he should never judge anyone else by their appearances.

Their angels have pushed them to the learning

experiences, and from there have shaped Dan and Jim's spirituality and guided their personas into new ways of being. This part of the process is very important because when the nudges from Past Life Angels are strong enough and irresistible enough to encourage humans to truly become conscious of themselves, the aspiration to evolve spiritually manifests itself in whatever form is the more powerful. The next task of the angel is to make the being "directionalize" its awakening towards an ever-higher level of development. This means that the nudges will not stop at the first sign of dawning memories, or even when a more profound spirituality is attained, but will continue to prompt for the rest of the being's life.

This is because it's important that human beings not only accept the impulses that start to drive them, and follow those signals, but also discover a deep sense of responsibility and care, not only for themselves but also for the rest of the conscious Universe. In this way they will become a pure expression and "causitory" agent for "God's" will, thus fulfilling their primary role.

CHAPTER 7

phobias, obsessions, and déjà vu

Phobias, Obsessions, and Déjà Vu

Another common way in which Past Life Angels get us to remember our spiritual part is by way of phobias. There are, of course, many phobias that can be easily explained. If you were frightened by something as a child, you might well retain a phobia of it as an adult. If you have a phobia of snakes or spiders or air travel, this might well be explained as a natural fear of creatures that could harm, or a potentially dangerous form of travel. But, there are many other phobias that either cannot be explained by a childhood experience, or are so strange that there doesn't seem to be a logical reason for the fear.

CATHY'S REGRESSION

Take, for instance, the case of Cathy. She wrote to me because a rather strange phobia was blighting her life. Her fear was of white statues. Nothing in her childhood could explain it and no amount of conventional therapy could cure it. She had tried everything, except paying attention to what her Past Life Angel was trying to tell her, because she didn't know that such a thing existed.

As Cathy grew up, the phobia, which had started at age five, got steadily worse. The other children thought it was funny to torment her, once pushing her into a statue of a horse. She soon had to avoid going anywhere that had white statues. She was fine with bronzes and anything else but white. Someone once suggested to her that this was past-life related, and so for a while the fear eased a little. I imagine her angel thought she had done enough. But Cathy didn't do anything about it untill 2003, when she and her husband went to York Minster, and she had a terrible incident there. She was sweating and crying "like a baby."

I sent her to see Janet Thompson, a hypnotherapist who is excellent at delving into your previous history and bringing answers for you up to your conscious mind. Cathy related an amazing story that explained everything:

It was happening again. The trip to York Minster with my husband was meant to be a treat, but I cowered, sweating and crying like a baby, transfixed with fear by the big white statue that towered over me. Ever since I was a child it had been the same. Other children thought it was funny to torment me, once pushing me into a statue of a horse. I wrote to Madeleine at *Chat It's Fate* to see if she could help me make any sense of my fear. She sent me to see a regression therapist – Janet Thompson in Hove.

Janet guided me into hypnosis and I quickly found myself inside a small, dark building. I knew it was my home, and I knew the house was in Rome some centuries ago. I told Janet that I lived there with my mother. Janet asked me what I did with my time and I found myself telling her that I worked in a place that had a lot of columns and big statues. I shuddered at the thought. The people there were rich and they made unkind and hard masters. I had to take my baby with me every day, because there was no one else to look after my tiny son.

Janet moved me forward, and suddenly I was filled with terror. I was at my place of work and the ground was moving. Big holes were opening all around me and I struggled to stay on my feet, screaming with fear. I tried to cover my baby's face as I desperately searched for a way out amid the swirling, choking clouds of dust that filled the air. I could hear the sounds of stone crashing to the ground and shards cut into me. I looked up and saw with horror that a massive statue was toppling over onto me. There was a sudden impact and everything went dark.

I cried out, "It killed me! Where's my baby? My baby!"

Janet soothed me, saying, "Just let your spirit leave that body and hover around, and look down from above. Look down without fear and just observe the details. Tell me what you can see. Can you see your body?"

I could just see my feet and one of my arms sticking out from underneath the rubble. I couldn't see my baby.

Janet said, "Just let yourself look to the side of you and see the spirit of your baby."

Suddenly I could feel him back in my arms. I sobbed with relief and held him tightly, knowing that we were together in spirit.

Janet reassured me, "So he's quite safe now. You are both quite safe now. When you are ready just let your spirit leave that lifetime and all that belongs in the past. Let you and your baby ascend into the light.

Janet guided me into the light and I met with my soul group and my primary spirit guide. She told me to ask for some understanding of that life and its karmic connections with this life. I was told by my guide that I needed to go and touch a white statue and then I would know that my fear was gone.

I couldn't believe how uplifted I felt. That very day I was able to walk into a shop and look through a book on sculptures, for the first time in this life, without panicking. I then went to a garden center and am now planning a trip to the British Museum and then St Paul's Cathedral.

Her angel must have been jumping for joy, because now that Cathy has 'woken up' she will be more receptive to remembering her whole self and this have a knock-on effect throughout her whole life.

CHRISTINE'S REGRESSION

This next case is probably the one with the most special interest to me personally. A woman called Chris wrote to me at the magazine and told me of her terrible agoraphobia. She desperately wanted to find out what had caused it and how she could get over it. It was one case where I decided to communicate with my own Past Life Angel, Jayella, and try to discover where Chris' phobia had come from.

This was what I told her afterwards:

In one of your lifetimes you were a sonar operator on board a submarine. I think this was in wartime. I also think that the submarine was torpedoed and cracked open. After months of being cooped up inside the sub, in a confined space, you were catapulted into the ocean, alone. Everyone else was trapped inside the submarine. The fear of endless blue all around, and nobody in sight, as the stricken sub plunged into the dark depths below, must have been horrifying. I think you died alone on the surface of the sea. There was no one, and nothing, anywhere to be seen. This *would* explain your problem. What we need to do is get you regressed back there, and then it can be healed. Even knowing the cause of your panic might help. Try and rationalize your fear now, knowing that you are *not* at sea, and you are *not* alone, and that there are people who can help you, whereas they couldn't back then."

This was Christine's reply:

> Well you certainly made me sit up when I read your letter! The part about me being alone at sea especially, because whenever I have been near our River Hull I get a horrible feeling inside, and if I see water, like oceans or seas, I get a really strange uncomfortable feeling of fear... I always say to whoever has been with me that I personally think that in my past life I probably drowned, and that's why I fear rivers or oceans. That is so true and now I understand why I get that awful feeling.

I sent her to see therapist Steve Burgess, and after treating Christine, this is what he had to say:

> Christine's case has actually been quite a complex one. Although I've been primarily focussing on the agoraphobia, treating it has been complicated by the fact that she has something I call "multiple phobia syndrome," in which several phobias all intertwine and enmesh themselves around the root cause emotions which have been locked in to cause the phobias in the first place. So, closely connected to the agoraphobia have been claustrophobia, dental phobia, needle phobia, spider phobia, as well as panic attacks and a strong fear of driving. All of these have their roots in past traumas in both this life and past lives.
>
> As we have been working on one phobia, another

one has from time to time become predominant, so we've had to take a side-step and work on the problem presenting itself, instead of just the agoraphobia. Although traumas in this life have played a part in causing her phobias and have had to be worked on to clear the negative emotions attached to them, several past lives have so far been uncovered and either fully or partly released. As a result, this has had a substantial impact on Chris and she is now showing signs of improvement in several areas.

With reference to the agoraphobia, as you know Chris was unable to go very far from her home at all without becoming panicky and anxious and having to return home immediately. As a result of our sessions, even though the agoraphobia is not fully cleared, she has gone further afield in the past few weeks than she has been able to do for some time. She has been able to go shopping along streets she has not been on for at least seven years. She has been able to go to a pub for a drink (and she said that during her evening in the pub she felt "free"). She has re-visited childhood haunts and even attended a wedding reception! Just this last week she managed to come to my office for her session with me – a real first, as so far I've been visiting her at home as she'd been unable to come into the city center. As you'd expect, she was a little tense but she came through the experience with flying colors.

As to the dental and needle phobia, she has traveled several miles to visit a dentist for a check-up and has booked an appointment for a tooth extraction, things she could not have contemplated doing a little while ago.

Her past lives have been quite traumatic. In the first one, she was a survivor of the destruction of Atlantis, alone and devastated by the disaster. The dental/needle phobia was caused by being imprisoned and horribly tortured, with much of the torture taking place in her mouth and her teeth. The past life which you'd intuited has also come through, in which she survives the blowing-up of a submarine in which she was a sailor in WWII, but is left floating alone on the surface of a vast, endless sea before she drowns.

Naturally, when I read this very last part I was gratified to see that the past life Jayella had communicated to me had come through, giving me verification that my message had been real. Chris is continuing to make progress as she works through her past lives and starts to make this one work better for her. ❖

The opposite of a phobia might be said to be an obsession. This can be another trigger used by your angel. People with this kind of a nudge going on often become avid collectors. I'm not talking about investors who build collections that are only for their monetary worth. The kind of person who is having a nudge will be one who devotes their whole life to collecting items either from a period in time, or those associated with a particular person or place.

The classic name for this is "gathering the familiar." What happens is that a person gets comfort from these places or items because they feel familiar. We all like to be surrounded with familiarity and it qualifies as a past life nudge when we get that comfort from something we have had no experience of in this lifetime.

I met Dr Ian Baillie a few years ago when he was a guest on my TV show. His story, told in full in his book *Rebel Spirit*, is a very good example of '"gathering the familiar."

From quite a young age Ian was obsessed with the American Civil War. He even spent months as a boy creating a perfect replica of the Confederate Flag and a working rifle of the period. He collected everything he could from the time of the war and thought of little else all through his childhood, constantly playing out the same battle scenes over and over again with his toy soldiers.

His obsession continued unabated into adulthood. He became a physicist and decided to make it his life's work to uncover the mysteries of subconscious memories, and how they survive death, after the coincidental discovery of an old photograph in a book on the American Civil War. The book dropped at his feet from a bookstore shelf and opened on the page bearing a photograph of another Baillie. Ian discovered to his astonishment that he had not only the same name as the soldier in the picture but also the same face.

This triggered his subconscious memory into unlocking, and further research found irrefutable evidence that the battles he had re-enacted as a child were actual crucial events from the previous Baillie's days with the 5th Georgia Cavalry. So, Ian was able to clearly demonstrate the fact that our conscious emotional memory survives physical mortality. He was able to show conclusively that intense emotion is the language of subconscious memory and that our everyday existence in the physical plane is often dramatically being controlled by our own personal cryptic agenda – or master plan.

Ian was able to unlock the romantic story of a secret love affair on the coastal tidewater of antebellum Georgia at the time of the American Civil War. Images he had always had in his mind of innocent aristocratic beauty, long blonde hair, and an image of a lighthouse, also all played their part as key subliminal factors in the triggering of events throughout Ian's present life, and thus made another bridge from the present to the past. It seems that Ian, like me, was destined to remember a particular past life for reasons that have cosmic implications and so his nudges, like mine, were persistent and ultimately irresistible.

The shock realization eventually dawned on Ian that the entire story of his past life as Baillie was being re-enacted by the people that surrounded him in his current life. So not only was this just the personal past-life memory of a single being, but an exciting insight into the workings of the physical matrix that we call our world, demonstrating how soul clans come together as spiritual beings, using their earthly journey to solve past emotional trauma.

This, for Ian, was to be the crowning achievement of twenty years' work into understanding the true nature of consciousness, space, and time. An insight that just had to be shared with the world and it is no coincidence that this is entirely *coincidental* with the present phase in the evolution of our home planet and its spiritual future. Ian's story may be the key scientific evidence that universal intelligence wants stories such as his to be publicly known at this present time. This kind of evidence will contribute to humanity's continued spiritual evolution. ❖

This brings me to the phenomenon known as déjà vu. In fact, there are several different kinds of déjà vu, more than you might think.

There is the dictionary definition: Déjà vu: Literally translates to "already seen." In English the term is associated with seeing or doing something entirely new, but having the distinct feeling that the experience had been done before. However, this can be split into four subcategories:

Déjà lu: Literally translates to feeling as if you have already read something before.

Déjà visite: A feeling of having already been somewhere before.

Déjà senti: A feeling of having experienced a sensation or emotion before.

Déjà vecu: Having a feeling of having done something before.

I believe there are cases of being mistaken when it comes to incidences of déjà vu. There are many hypotheses put forward to account for it. One of these can be due to the theory of parallel time – whereby someone can momentarily see across the time lines seconds before the actual event – in the same way that clairvoyants can. Also, the same can apply in cases of déjà vu, but in the case of someone who can accurately describe a place they have never been to, as in déjà visite, then there is no doubt in my mind that Past Life Angels are at work.

The most famous case of the several past life aspects of what is collectively called "déjà vu," and one which has been extensively recorded, is that of Shanti Devi. Shanti was born in 1926 in India. Her mother was worried about the child because she often seemed to be confused, and when she was 7 she told her mother that she used to live in a town called Muttra, which was some distance away from their hometown of Delhi. Shanti described the town, the house where she said she had lived, and her family. She said that all this had taken place in another lifetime.

All the time she was growing up, Shanti never changed her story and her parents started to think that she was mentally ill, although doctors could not find anything wrong with her. At the age of nine she added to the story, saying that when she had lived in Muttra, she had been married and had three children. She even named them, and went on to say that her own name in that life had been Ludgi.

One day, a strange man knocked on the door of the family home. Shanti got very excited and claimed that the man was the cousin of her husband in her previous life. The man did live in Muttra, but had only come to the house to talk business with Shanti's father. (Or had been sent there?) He told Shanti's parents that his cousin had lost his wife, Ludgi, some ten years earlier.

When he was told the whole of Shanti's claims, the man said he would get his cousin to travel to Delhi to meet her. Shanti's parents didn't tell her of this plan, wanting to see if she would know the man when he arrived. When he came, Shanti immediately threw herself into his arms, crying and saying that he was her husband.

Shanti was taken to Muttra. As well as knowing the layout of the town, where she had lived, and the people, Shanti also started speaking in the local dialect.

KAREN'S REGRESSION

Karen showed an example of another typical past life nudge. In her case her angel used déjà visite. She used to love country walks, and one in particular ended with a walk along a disused railway line. Karen could never understand why this part of the walk always filled her with unease. She felt she knew the place and that it didn't have a happy feeling for her.

She went to see regressionist Dave Goodfellow, to see if he could shed some light on why she felt so uncomfortable on that part of her walk. Between them they soon got to the bottom of things.

My name was Prudence and I was eighteen years old. I found myself playing croquet by the river. There was a huge lawn in the grounds of a grand house, which had a broad veranda and steps. To my left were my aunt and sister, and to my right my brother and his friend. I wasn't any good at the game, but I was still better than my brother. He didn't like that, as girls were supposed to giggle and get it wrong. Nanny said it was time for tea, so we went back to the terrace to eat. My brother wasn't very happy with me as I beat him, but I didn't care and thought it served him right. I knew that the house was near Leeds, although I'd never been there, and that my father was something important in the railways and the coal industry.

Dave moved me forward and I found myself sitting in the grounds, under a tree, on a kind of bench shaped around the trunk. I was reading a book. My father's brother came along, as I knew he would. He wasn't at all nice. He wanted me to put the book down. He didn't really want to talk to me. I wanted to leave.

He touched my shoulder, and said, "Don't go." He made me squirm. "I've got to go," I insisted. He chased me, and the grass was slippery. I fell on the grass and my face was wet and covered in mud. He came up behind me and he hurt me. He was a vicious old man. He really hurt me. I couldn't tell anyone, because to talk of such things was indecent. I was bleeding between my legs, and he just walked away. I went to the house and to my room and wash and scrub myself. I washed and scrubbed more and more. The water was too cold and didn't wash anything away.

My uncle's name was Arthur Brown. He lived in the village. He had a nice house – it was a gatehouse. I'd like to live there. When I was a child I used to visit him there and his wife died. She was nice. She used to give me little flat cakes with butter and jam. Her name was Ellis.

Dave took me forward again and I was lying down in the chapel grounds. I was dead, but I wasn't in the box, I was floating above, looking down on the people who were looking into my coffin. I knew that I'd died in childbirth, giving birth to the baby my uncle had forced on me along with his abuse.

That didn't seem to be the life that involved my current problem with the railway path, so Dave took me on to another one.

This time I was a man. I was twenty-four years old and I lived in Bradford, with my wife, Ellen, and two children, Charlie and a three-month-old baby, Katie. It was 1912, and I was walking along a street in wet and nasty weather. I worked in a shoe factory, Lowther and Son, and I was on my way there. I lived at 21, Canal Road, two blocks down, and the house had come with the job. It was hard for me and Ellen to earn enough money to feed the children. I was very quick at my job so I averaged three guineas. I hated my job and skived off down the pub whenever I could get away with it.

I moved forward to a time when I was telling off my young son, Charlie, for playing on the railway line. He was always doing it, no matter that I'd told him fifty times not to. Inevitably, in the end, Charlie was run over by a train. It took his head clean off. After we buried Charlie, I could see no point in living anymore. I only had a daughter – lost my only son, and I didn't care about anything. I wanted to die, so I went down to the railway line. I lay down with my head on the rails, looking at the spot where they'd found Charlie's head. I could feel the rails vibrate as the train approached. I was very relaxed.

Because Dave Goodfellow had put in the proper safeguards, Karen was able to ask to come out of the session at this point. With appropriate healing Dave ended the session. Karen says that since the session she has walked along the same route with no problem, and although she now feels slightly emotional there, she's not uncomfortable.

Releasing this kind of pent-up trauma always has a lasting effect on the rest of the client's life, and quite often they will soon go on to change other areas of their lives as they start to remember what they came here for. This new knowledge also gives their angels a "head-start" in the next lifetime, if another life is necessary, when it comes to trying to wake them up again.

communication with past life angels

Communication with Past Life Angels

You can see that finding out about your past can have far-reaching consequences, and knowing this will help you understand what your spiritual guardian – your Past Life Angel – is trying to tell you, and why it is so important that you listen.

The easiest and most accurate way that a Past Life Angel can communicate with you, is by way of meditation, but there are many kinds of meditation. A lot of people say they don't or can't meditate. This is a fallacy; because everybody meditates, intentionally or not. We are bound to, because our subconscious never entirely sleeps, whereas our conscious mind does. I'm not talking about dreams at this point though, or, if they are dreams, I would call them waking dreams. These moments of involuntary meditation can happen in several different ways.

Have you ever been driving your car along a familiar road, and then suddenly found you have no recollection of travelling the last few miles? You suddenly realize that you have safely negotiated several roundabouts and turnoffs, but you have no memory of the actual details. I'm sure you have. This means you have been meditating.

Have you ever been standing, doing the washing up, and then just drifted off into some kind of thoughtless place? Have you ever been reading a book, and then had to read the same page again, because you have no idea what you just read? All of these times, and many others you can think of when you went "somewhere else" for a while, are examples of involuntary meditation.

I have a little trick I use in this regard to try and show people how they can meditate, even if they think it's impossible for them. Meditating is merely the closing down of all conscious thought – whether you let the cat out, are going to be late home, forgot an item of shopping, etc., so that the subconscious will have a chance to speak without being drowned out by these things. When someone tells me that they cannot do it, and that they find it impossible to shut out their everyday lives and worries enough to find that still and silent place within, I ask them to hold and gaze at a fluorite crystal for a few moments without trying to switch off at all. If you are someone who finds meditating difficult, give this a try.

I mention to the person how the colors in a piece of fluorite seem to flow and melt, and how there seem to be rivers and oceans and whole worlds inside the swirling greens and purples. Then I wait a couple of minutes and ask the person, "What are you thinking about?" "Em… nothing really," they reply sleepily. Voila! Meditation!

During these times our angels must snatch the chance to communicate if they can, and they do this in a variety of ways. You might see brief flashes of visions at those times, or hear a few words that seem to be in someone else's voice. You might get a strong feeling of somebody you haven't seen for a long time, or come out of the daze with a feeling that we should do something, or contact someone. Very creative people will use these flashes of insight to enhance their performances, and creative writers in particular have been known to draw on them for inspiration.

If this happens, try and make a note of what you see or hear, because eventually a pattern will appear and you'll be able to figure out the entire message. If you are led to meet someone you haven't seen for a while, take special interest in what they have to say. Brief visions can be very compelling, and if they are, you can be sure they are from your angel. I've had some wonderful examples of these from my readers. For instance, one man wrote this to me:

> One morning a few weeks ago, I was sitting alone, and I found myself looking down a short tunnel. At the bottom lay an old-fashioned horn beaker bound with silver strapwork. It was on its side and empty, but light was falling on it from somewhere and made it sparkle brilliantly. I felt ecstatic looking at this.

This was a great effort on behalf on the man's angel. When visions like this come in the waking hours, it probably means that countless signs have been ignored and the angel is getting desperate to get through to the person.

Another way that these angels can reach you is to come to you in proper dreams. In my case, I suffered from terrible nightmares. They were, as any that are sent by your angel will be, repetitive. I always say that if anything happens three times or more, then it's a message, as if jumping up and down for your attention. It might seem a little cruel to send messages in the form of nightmares that really terrify, but when you consider what is at stake, i.e. your whole spiritual future, you really can't blame the angels for using anything they can if they are having trouble getting through. I realize now that my angel had been trying to "wake me up" for forty-five years. I can also see in hindsight that my Past Life Angel could see circumstances approaching that it could use for my further education, if it could get me into the right frame of mind to take advantage of them.

So, how do you tell the difference between ordinary dreams and nightmares, and past life nudges? Any dream or nightmare can be emotional. You might wake up crying or laughing. Sometimes dreams can seem so real that you can't believe they were not. But past life dreams, sent by your angels, are quite different. With a normal dream, once you wake up, or at least by later in the day, you are over the emotion. The things that scared or delighted you are just vague memories, but with a genuine past life dream you will never get over the emotions it brought to you.

Days, weeks, or years later the emotions of the dream or nightmare will still be as powerful as they were before and you will laugh or cry as you did at the time of the dream. The memory will be as real and as abiding as your memories of this life, because that's exactly what they are – real.

It doesn't matter if you are awake or asleep when these flashes happen. Some people have had spontaneous memories come to them while just walking along. Of course in those instances you have to be "switched off" enough for your angel to get through to you.

For years I had a recurrent dream, and I used to believe it must be a precognition. It was about a house and I used to tell everyone that, one day, I would be living in this house – it was the only reason I could think of at the time. The house was a period property; I believe it was Georgian. It was red brick built, large and imposing, and I recall very clearly that there were stables between it and the black railings that separated it from the roadside. Inside the house there was a very pleasant arrangement of rooms, and between living areas there was a step down into a beautifully lit area with large curving glass doors at the end. In this room there was a chest of drawers that had been made into a plant holder. There was also a bookcase and I felt behind the books to discover a small white silk flower, which I had obviously known was there. Upstairs the rooms had slopes in their ceilings, and there were huge walk-in cupboards that ran between some of the rooms, in the eaves.

It took years for it to dawn on me that this wasn't a dream of the future, but a memory of the past. I am sure now that one day I will find this house, and I feel that the white silk flower was placed there by me deliberately in some other life, so that I would have proof once I rediscovered the house. This is the kind of dream that is sent to you by your Past Life Angel.

It doesn't always have to be a nightmare, and it doesn't always have to be when you are in REM sleep. There is a state called the "hypnogogic" that we all pass through, either on our way into, or our way out of, sleep. Your angel will usually try and get through just as you are dozing off. The byword is that it takes twenty minutes to get into true REM sleep, so any "dream" you have before that time, might not be a dream at all, it might be a message.

The hypnogogic state that this kind of message has access to, is the same condition that yogis are adept at reaching deliberately, and is a deeply meditative state. We can achieve it quite naturally, but of course we're not making full use of it most of the time, because we haven't realized what it is. It's a great way to start to understand what real meditation is like, and you can begin to train yourself to receive messages by using it. When you prepare to go to bed, put a pen and paper next to your bed in easy reach. Set your alarm clock to go off fifteen minutes later, and when it does, quickly write down everything you can remember. (Trust me, you'll forget it otherwise, or at least your conscious mind will.)

Of course, at first you may find you have difficulty drifting off, just because you want to, and because you are waiting for the alarm clock to go off, but if you practice more and more you will soon train yourself to relax as a part of your routine, which will be very good for you anyway. If you find it really impossible, try counting your breaths. Start at a number that is not easy, such as 371, and count backwards, one for each breath. If you find yourself coming round or thinking off track, just start again, being sure to write down anything that goes through your mind. (My Past Life Meditation CD might help you with this.) If you can learn to concentrate on the numbers and the breaths and that's all, I guarantee that you will drift off. It might take practice to learn to concentrate, but it will happen if you persevere.

Some cynical people will immediately label this kind of thing "imagination." They may well be right, but ask those same people a question, "What *is* imagination? Define it." They will not have an answer that doesn't involve the words, "subconscious" or "higher mind," or "power of the mind" or some such thing that will place "imagination" into the spiritual realm. It cannot be quantified or explained. The same applies to "love." Cynics cannot explain that phenomenon either. It is not a scientific manifestation. They can explain chemical attraction, but that it not the same as love. So these two words, "imagination" and "love," have no sensible explanation other than the spiritual.

I'm often asked how you can tell the difference between a normal dream, and that which relates to a past life. The answer is the same as the one to the questions, "How do you know past life memories under hypnosis are real?" and "How do you know you're not just remembering a film you saw, or a book you read?" The difference lies in the emotional content and the emotional durability. If you watch a sad or uplifting film or read a sad book, or even see a very inspiring or tragic real-life story on the news, it will get to you, perhaps making you cry with grief or with happiness. If you have a good or frightening dream, the same will apply. But with any of these cases the fear, sorrow, or happiness will fade within hours if not minutes. With a genuine memory of an event that happened to you in another life, you will never completely shake those emotional responses. The memory will continue to elicit those same strong feelings in you whenever you think of them, just like they would if they were a memory from this lifetime.

Astral travel or out-of-body experiences can also cross over into past life signals. I had conclusive proof of this myself, although what happened might be considered as anecdotal by others. If you are someone who has lived in many different houses, you might perhaps have experienced waking up and not knowing for a few seconds which house you are currently in. Well, I woke up one morning and for about thirty seconds I did not know which body I was in. It was quite frightening for a moment, but then I *felt* Tony's soul next to me, and I thought, "Oh, I'm Jenny." I didn't think, "Oh, I'm me" – but "Jenny." That my conscious mind chose to think in the third person, rather than the first, spoke volumes to me.

Slowly, what I had been "dreaming" came back to me. I had been visiting a previous lifetime. I recognized it from a regression I had once done. What had then happened was that, as I woke suddenly, the lives from that one to this were "leafed through," almost like playing cards, as I tried to choose the right current life. I also had a tantalizing and frustrating knowledge that just before I woke up I had all the "answers" in front of me. Answers to everything. But, as they always do, the answers slipped away just as sleep did. At least I had confirmed for me, once again, that our subconscious does indeed know all the answers, and that there is so much more to us, as beings, than we seem to be able to comprehend.

Another common angelic use of involuntary meditation is that of patterns. Some people find themselves drawn to patterns. They become transfixed staring at patterns in crystals, paintings, or even carpets or curtains, etc, and this leaves their minds open to visions. They will see faces in the patterns that will start to repeat, perhaps in wallpaper or leaves. They will come finally to accept that this face they are seeing must be from their memories and, if this happens, the Past Life Angel will chalk it up as at least a partial success.

Your sense of smell can be utilized by your angel. Of all our senses, that of smell is the one that is most effective as a memory-jogger. An angel will create a certain smell as a reminder of the past. So, if you sometimes smell something for no apparent reason, sit and think quietly about what the scent brings to mind, because you'll probably find it was a major clue to your past.

One way in which I have often received communication from my Past Life Angel is with automatic writing. Any kind of meditation will do for this: deliberate or involuntary, as long as you either have a pen in your hand, or are sitting at the keyboard. All you need to do is to hand over control of the keyboard or pen to your higher self. It must be clear by now that any form of "switching off" the conscious mind can give your angel access to your unconscious.

Creative ability is another way that clues can be passed to you. This can sometimes take the form of what is called psychic art. People who normally have no artistic talent can, under certain conditions, produce stunning artwork. They will often do using their non-dominant hand, so a right-handed person will do the psychic art using their left hand. The artwork can be abstract and the images revealed personal to the artist, or they can clearly depict scenes from past lives.

One final way that angels have of communicating past lives is with intuition or psychic ability. The first time I found myself able to see what *other peoples'* past life angels were trying to show them was at a concert hall in Belfast. The artist performing was Garth Brooks, the man who shared a past life with me in the 1600s as Ryan. I'd gone there in an attempt to talk to Garth and my friend, and member of my soul clan, Graham Goodall was with me. Graham had decided to stand further back from the stage, to see better, while I was near the front, so we were several feet apart. At one point during the concert a strange thing happened. I saw Garth's clothes shimmer and change into those he would have worn in the 1600s, as Ryan. He literally changed before my eyes into Ryan. I was stunned by this and transfixed. The next moment there was a hand on my shoulder and I realized Graham had chosen that moment to stand behind me.

Later, he explained that he had seen Garth change into Ryan and, worrying slightly as to the effect this might have had on me, he'd come to be next to me. It was amazing and of course very validating that Graham had seen what I'd seen. It may seem odd that the rest of the audience didn't share our vision, but of course both of us were connected to "Ryan" and they were not.

The second time this happened was when we both met Garth on a personal level. My husband, Tony, was there too, and all three of us noticed Garth change once more into Ryan. The validation this time, should we have needed more, was that during this time, Garth said some extraordinary things. Stars have, by necessity, to keep certain things about themselves private but, at the time Garth became Ryan, all barriers went down, and he told us with entire honesty and openness things that would have had the press jumping with glee if we had repeated them. Needless to say, we never did. Violating that trust would have been unforgivable.

After that time it happened more regularly and with stronger effects, until today, when I am often able to see other peoples' angel messages, even without being in the same place as them. I think my Past Life Angel has realized that he can "network" this way, which, of course, can be a big help to everyone concerned. It often does happen though when I am with someone. I have seen peoples' clothes change into crinoline dresses, farm laborer's smocks, and baggy trousers, and sometimes I get feelings and action to go with the clothes.

One lady I saw wearing a woolen dress and clogs, and she was walking up a cobble-stoned hill, carrying a basket of apples in her hands. I could see that it was misty and the surroundings looked like a medieval village. She immediately told me that she'd seen that lifetime herself, and it was one in which she had been killed by her own son.

CHAPTER 9

family circles

Family Circles

This brings me to family circles (and I *do* mean circles), which are a problem all of their own. Some families seem to be tied together life after life. You might think this would make the relationships between them solid and easy, but this isn't the case. It's easy to see why when you consider that in order for the soul to learn and progress it has to experience a wide gamut of emotional situations. This means that almost like an acting troupe touring the country together, the members of the group will be required to have different roles depending on the "play" they're performing.

So, imagine that six lifetimes ago your father was your daughter, your mother was your brother and your son was your grandfather and so on. If all goes well, which really it rarely can, human nature being what it is, then things will have progressed smoothly and in this life there will be no problems. What normally happens, of course, is that there are conflicts, feuds, abuse, lies, deception, incest, and, just occasionally, harmony. This means that most of the time there is a whole stack of unfinished business, attaching itself like fleas to the back of every lifetime.

As with relationships in general, once in spirit the group communicates together and devises plans to make sure that in the next lifetime everything is sorted out and all the souls can achieve their objectives. But of course once we are here, facing the repetitive challenge of remembering it all (by uniting body, mind, and soul completely), we usually fail miserably. Things get ever more complicated father who was husband might perhaps have very confused emotions and previous dislikes and hurts and intimacy from previous relationships can all get in the way. Thus things get more and more complex and in the end can be almost impossible for the individual to unravel. All or any of these things going on means that the parties concerned are getting nudges, which should not be ignored.

In a case like this, it's quite important to seek the help of a qualified therapist. If this is done, the therapist can work with all of the group's Past Life Angels, and by using them as guides, the mysteries and complexities can be sorted out, and a new pathway laid out for the family. But this, of course, depends on at least most, if not all of the members being ready to listen to their own angels. What can help with this is if two or more family members come up with the same past life scenario, which can be used (if a tape recording has been made) to convince other members to join in with the investigation. In cases like this the therapist needs to be not only an excellent one, but also something of a past life detective, and definitely one who is used to working with the angels of their clients. You can see then that family groups are probably the hardest to sort out, and are often the most troublesome because of it.

Sometimes you might not have even been in the same family with someone causing you problems in this life's family group. What does happen though, is that we tend to re-enact scenarios over and over with the same people. You can see how someone who perceives that you did them wrong in a past life might make things difficult for you this time around, and if they turn up this time as a close family member, you can have big problems. If course the *intention* will have been to sort things out this time around, and not perpetuate the difficulties but, sadly, that's not too often what happens.

There is a saying, "You choose your friends but you can't choose your family." In fact the reverse is true – you do in fact choose your family. This can be difficult to understand, especially if you don't get on with them. But everything and everyone are carefully selected to give you the opportunity to build bridges, make up for past mistakes, learn new behavior patterns, and finish unfinished business. It's all a lot easier if it's within the same group of people.

I have two beautiful examples of how family circles can cause never-ending repetitive problems if they are not addressed.

CASE ONE

A woman called Maria went to see Dutch therapist, Anita Groenendijk, because she couldn't get on with her family. She got very nervous when they visited her, and she said, "My hair stands on end when they show up here, because I feel so threatened by them." She admitted she had never felt safe with her family. The biggest problem she had was with her mother. Her mother was ill a lot, had epileptic episodes, and could not handle normal day-to-day household chores. She quickly took her anger out on her daughter, and hit her frequently. Maria did all the household tasks at home from the age of six. She was mostly raised by her grandma, who was very sweet to her. Apart from those moments full of love with her grandmother, Maria was denied the chance to be a child. Her father had a weak character and was totally subservient to Maria's mother's wishes. He never stood up for his children.

Maria was afraid of losing her mind, because she couldn't control herself anymore, and could never find quietness in herself. During the conversation with Anita she said she was also very afraid that she might turn out like her mother. She also showed that she is very angry at her mother, but in a repressed way. She felt her family had let her down in a major way, and that they didn't appreciate what she had done for them since her childhood. Apart from that, she was having great difficulty letting go of her own son, who wanted to leave home. What she would really like was to be able to relax again, and live an easier life. Her self-esteem was very low, and she would never dare to speak in public.

During the first session, she appeared to be overloaded with emotions and energy, which had come from her problems with her mother and the rest of her family. She had always felt very responsible for their well-being, and had taken on all their troubles. Anita cleared this excess energy by visualization, breathing, and aura healing. Anita used the kinesiologic muscle test to check if everything was cleared and the patient was ready for therapy to continue. She also asked Maria to write a letter to her mother, in which she would tell her all the things she was angry and sad about, without actually sending the letter.

In the second session Maria told Anita that she felt quite good about herself, and that she felt her self-worth rise after writing the letter. She still felt very angry and upset with her mother though, and still felt nervous about family visiting her. In this session Anita guided Maria into regression, targeting it around this feeling of anger towards her mother. First, Maria went back in her current life, to the age of four. Her "Mommy" was in a fit of anger and took away her only toy, throwing it in the fire. Little Maria was terrified, sad, and beaten. She sighed, "I can't believe my own mother would do this kind of thing."

After instructing Maria to breathe out all the old emotions, Anita told her to take the child away and out of the situation. Under Anita's instruction Maria also blew away the angry words her mother said to her. Anita then asked Maria what little Maria needed. Maria saw a very kind schoolteacher she once had, and a sweet aunt. She says she felt warmth inside then. Maria was able to stop feeling anger and sadness, and she told Anita after the session that she felt lighter. In fact, she felt so good that she decided that she didn't need another session.

After the session everything went well for quite some time. Maria had more energy, her family didn't bother her anymore, there was no stress, and her self-esteem was relatively very good. But after five months she returned for another session.

She was furious again. During those five months she started to feel more and more anger towards her mother again. She felt she was the black sheep of the family. She was tired a lot and slow in the mornings. She said, "It's all too much for me now." Her

GP told her that it was just stress, and he couldn't help her with that.

When she talked about her mother she pointed at her chest, and said she felt suffocated. Anita decided that it was time to go back into Maria's past lives and work with her karmic connection with her mother.

It turned out there were five lives in which she interacted with the soul who is her present mother. Maria was a bit scared about past lives, but wanted to do it at the same time. In one session they looked at those lives in a chronological way, and where necessary healed past life trauma.

Their first life together was in Africa. It was an idyllic life; they belonged to a close group living in harmony with nature. Maria's past persona was part of this family group, and she was a woman. Her present mother was her child there. They had a very close connection, full of love and harmony. No trauma there.

The second life started very well for both Maria and her mother. They were two boys, Carlos and Giorgio, in a city in Italy, who played a lot together and became close friends. As an adult, Carlos (Maria) married Giorgio's (Maria's mother) sister, so they became even closer, and also related by marriage. Carlos was a baker, and his work at all hours and his large family took up all of his time. He had no more time for his friendship with Giorgio. Giorgio stayed childless, felt neglected, and became jealous of Carlos. After some time, he started to resent Carlos and their friendship deteriorated and died. When his former friend died, Carlos did not show up at his deathbed. Carlos was a very righteous man and did not feel he had wronged his friend. His conscience seemed clear.

Their next life was in North Africa, and was a nomad life. This time Maria was Frances and her mother was her husband, Simon. Simon was a jealous husband, who kept Frances on very short leash. He accused her of affairs with other men. He kept her imprisoned. Her parents had married her to him and so she'd had no choice. She did grow to love him in a way though; she never hated him.

Their next life they were only together very briefly. Maria lived nine months in her mother's womb as a male fetus, but due to the size of the baby's head and the woman's small pelvis, he couldn't be born alive. The mother couldn't let the boy child go. Maria moved away from this soul, but at the same time the heart connection grew between them.

Their last past life was different. It was at the start of the twentieth century. On a Greek island, Maria was Stephan, a married man with children. Stephan was an illegitimate son, and Maria's mother in this life was the legitimate son of the same man. So they were half-brothers, and Stephan's mother was married to another man. The fact that they were half-brothers was a secret. Stephan's mother revealed the secret when he was an adult, and he started to search for his father and brother, Paulo. He eventually finds Paulo, but the father had already died. To Stephan's disappointment, Paulo was not happy with the reunion. He forcefully rejects Stephan, telling him that he is a liar and that he wants nothing to do with him. Stephan felt very hurt and gets bitter, and stops trying to have contact anymore.

In her present life, Maria was born to her mother, and the

mother still rejects her with a vengeance, as Paulo did. It started when Maria turned out to be a girl. Her mother wanted a boy.

The line of events was clear. First they met, they loved each other, and then they drifted apart. Maria's mother wanted to stop that process and so tried to grab her too hard. This made Maria move away even more. Then it was hard for Maria to let go of her mother, even though she was treated really badly in her childhood. But under all those karmic layers of rejection, bitterness, and anger there was still the original love between them.

Maria needed to make contact with that love. At the end of the session Maria told Anita she now felt so much softer towards her mother. She said she understood how things came to pass, and accepted them, that she felt very relaxed and calm, and that her anger had disappeared. Maria saw she could not heal her mother's bitterness, and that all she could do was to love and accept her. They ended by making contact with Mother Earth, who could give Maria what her current mother was not able to give.

Several months after the session Maria called Anita to tell her she felt very good. She said she had a lot of energy, and had lost 20 kilos of weight. She said that her family didn't give her stress anymore, and there had even been reconciliations between every member. She would be able to let go of her son, and she had found a new love-partner in her life.

CASE TWO

Sue Phillips and her husband, Morgan, couldn't believe it. Not again! Her son, Jonathon, had dropped the family right into yet another financial quagmire. Their relationship was hitting rock bottom. It all started when Jonathon was twelve. Sue said, "I started to feel cross at him for no reason. I kept it from him because he was a good boy and I loved him, but the secret surges of anger I felt confused me."

By the time Jonathon was older, things had taken a serious tone. "He started spending money and getting me to take out loans on his behalf. As soon as the first couple of payments had gone through, he'd leave his job for a better one that never materialized, or would get ill, and I'd be left with the debt."

Jonathon seemed determined to bankrupt the family, and Sue believed he was out to destroy her. Time and time again Jonathon had landed the whole family in financial trouble.

And now the end had surely come. Sue says, "Jonathon was a warehouse manager and paying his bills, but one day when the ground was iron hard with frost, we were walking the dogs, and the biggest one knocked him over. He was thrown into the air and landed on his head. He suffered concussion, broken ribs, and a fracture of a bone in his chest. It was partly my fault, because I didn't call out a warning even when I saw the danger. I couldn't understand why I didn't warn my son."

Sue was at her wit's end. If only someone really wise could give her an answer. It took her some time to realize that she and Jon *did* have the answer, and the wisdom they sought was held within their souls.

She read somewhere that families could have problems due to past lives impinging on their present ones. Unraveling their past had solved their current-day problems. Were past lives real? She didn't know but, like a drowning man, Sue clutched at the tenuous straw. She decided to be regressed, ready to try anything.

Sue saw several lives under regression. She was a Celt woman, walking through a village, with a pair of dead chickens swinging from one hand. A man came at her from the darkness, and she only had time to see the flash of metal as an axe blazed towards her in a silvery arc. There was terrible pain, and then total darkness.

Then she found herself as a man on a field of war, with hordes of sword-wielding soldiers around her. She felt the heat of battle rage through her system, and bloodlust, terror, and anger gave her the strength to flail her heavy sword at the nearest enemy warrior. As he fell beneath her blow, the scene faded.

She found herself next in some kind of primitive courtroom in the 1600s. She was in the dock, men were shouting at her, and she felt scared and strangely befuddled. One man in particular seemed very angry at her for something she had just said, and as the scene disintegrated into violence she thought she recognized his face. Then she realized with horror that she was bound to a stake, and that there were flames licking around her feet. She screamed and choked on the smoke as it eddied around her. Through the smoky phantoms she glimpsed the angry man from the court being dragged past, and as he was hauled away he shouted at her that he never should have tried to help her. Just before she passed out she saw the man's face. It was Jonathon.

Discussing what she'd seen with Jonathon wasn't easy because he had no belief in such things, so she didn't go into detail. She was able to make him understand that all of their troubles might be a left-over from the past. She told him that maybe they could put them back in the past, where they belonged.

Days later Jonathon came to her with awe in his voice. He said that he'd started to have spontaneous flashes, as if what she had told him had opened some kind of doorway. He'd experienced murdering an old Celt woman with an axe. "Mum," he said, "I killed you!"

He'd seen himself on a battlefield, being run through by another warrior, and he'd recognized that warrior as Sue.

He'd been in the courtroom of her last regression. He told her: "I tried to defend you from the charges but you were so *stupid* that you implicated me, and I was killed too! I tried so hard that time to put things right, but you were an imbecile and you couldn't say what I told you to. That's why I've been so angry with you."

Mother and son stared at each other, a dawning awareness growing. They had literally been taking turns at destroying each other, over and over again. They were stuck on a merry-go-round of destruction, unable to stop. It explained everything. They knew they had to stop it, but how? They decided that a formal apology and forgiveness of each other must take place. They spoke the words to each other in a ceremonial fashion, "I forgive you for all you have done to me in the past, and I ask your forgiveness for all I have done to you."

Sue is still paying off the final debts that Jonathon incurred, but, as she says, "At least I have my son back, and from now on things can only get better." Sue's husband, Morgan, says, "I am very happy to see things change. It's been terrible seeing the two of them tear each other apart for so long." ❖

These are very good examples of how convoluted family relationships can become, and why help is often needed to unravel the entire tangled web. You can see how each time around between Maria and her mother there was the potential and the intention to engineer a situation for resolution and healing. Unfortunately, as nearly always happens, good intentions fade with time and emotional angst. If your Past Life Angel is sending you any nudges about your family circle, you really should take some action.

non-blood relationships

Non-Blood Relationships

SOUL MATES

Relationships are often a very tricky area. It's very easy to become confused about soul mates for instance. As humans we are naturally drawn to the familiar, and this is where the confusion happens. Quite often someone will be convinced that their partner is their soul mate, but then they get very unhappy because they can't understand why the relationship is still not working out. The problem can be that they are drawn to the person, not as they think, out of deep unending love, but because they are *familiar* to them.

Because of this, people often stick by someone, when in fact they were only drawn by the comforting feeling of familiarity, because subconsciously they recognize them from a past life. People have even ended up married to an old enemy, and this of course can bring up untold distress. The situation can be even more complex than that, because this old enemy and the person they are involved with might in fact have decided to be partners in this life, just so that the "old enemy" can make amends for the past.

Also, someone might in fact be a soul mate, but not be destined to be a partner this time around. Quite often a past life soul mate will come into your life, just to give you a nudge (guided to do so by your and their Past Life Angels, or because they contracted to do so), onto your rightful path in life. People are often under the misconception that everyone only has one true soul mate, but this is not correct.

There are several different kinds of soul mate. There are those who come from your soul clan, who will always be there for you, cannot help themselves in fact, but are not meant to be a partner to you in the conventional sense. There are those who have been with you through many lives, and come into your life, often briefly, to offer help for a time. There are those who are destined to be your lover, and that is the perfect relationship.

So, how on earth do you tell whether you are with the right person or not? One way is to both be regressed. A talented therapist will be able to uncover past life relationships, and if they are very good, they might be able to uncover any contracts you made together while still in spirit. Some couples have used my Past Life Meditation CD together, and by comparing notes afterwards have not only proved to themselves that they did share previous lives together, but also triggered their subconscious minds into telling them what their agreement was for this time.

SOUL CLANS

Circles, like those with blood relatives, can also apply to other groups of people, and this can be a good or a difficult thing. When you met somebody for the first time and immediately felt really happy in their close company, without any gender-based, chemical reaction, then your Past Life Angel has guided them into your space so that you can get that nudge from recognizing them. Never ignore this kind of feeling.

One of the really nice ways that this can happen is with your soul clan. A soul clan is your spiritual family, or tribe. While in spirit, they work with your Past Life Angel, and their own of course, to plan and steer your life so that you can come away from it with what you need. Your soul clan can be members of your earthly family, or they can just be close friends. They can be living at the same time as you, or be in spirit. They will never be entirely in human form, any more than you are, but will always leave a part of themselves in spirit. Therefore you will always have allies in the spirit world. They can't actively involve themselves in your physical life, unlike the angels, but they can do something that can really make the difference to your "waking up," or not. A past life member of your soul clan who takes up physical form can leave a message for you with the group that is still in spirit, before they leave it.

This means that in the right circumstances, perhaps during a consultation with a medium, you can receive this message. The result of this can be a huge readiness to be "switched on," which leaves the door open for guidance from your Past Life Angel.

This is your real family, the one that has been and will always be with you and for you, on a soul level, no matter what experiences you are going through. This, of course, is because they understand why you are doing what you are doing, and being who you are being, because all of us, when we are in spirit, have the advantage of divine knowledge.

In comparison, your earthly family are merely players who interact with you in different lifetimes, in different roles, just like a troupe of travelling actors, and the group dynamic is totally different than with a soul clan. Sometimes though, you will find a member of your soul clan within your human family, and this is always a wonderful thing to have.

So, if you ever feel you are really alone, always know that you have a lot of good energy coming to you from your soul clan. The whole world may seem to be against you, but your soul clan never will be.

On the other hand, if someone's presence immediately fills you with a strong need to push them away, or leave, then the chances are your intuition has been kicked into play, because your angel is trying to warn you that this person was an enemy in the past. If this is the case your best bet is not to trust the person and to go with your feelings. However, there is one proviso. Past life enemies often arrange to interact with us because their intention is to make up for the past, and they need to have that chance. However, tread with caution even if you feel this is the case, because good intentions are not always carried through, once the person is back in human form, and unless the person is listening to their angel, old habits and patterns can re-establish themselves to your detriment.

Soul mates are another very confusing area. If you were with someone, closely and intimately in a past life, and you re-encounter them in your current one, the potential for problems is vast. This is because of the confusion that can arise. The comfort gained from familiarity can be confused with the comfort you get from being with someone you love.

The fact is that past life acquaintances, and even past life soul mates are not always meant to be together as partners, and the feeling you get from meeting one might be misconstrued by you as meaning that you are. It can be very difficult if you feel very strongly that you are meant to be with someone, when you are not. Mistakes can be heartbreaking and devastating. Sometimes two soul mates have made what is called a "contract" between them. This usually means that one of them promises the other that at a certain point in their lives, when they are desperately in need of a little guidance, the first one will enter the second one's life, briefly, just to give them a signpost to follow, which will lead them in the right direction.

Unfortunately this act can be taken as a sign of deep and abiding love by the second person, and they can then mistakenly waste a lot of valuable time chasing after a red herring, believing that they are pursuing eternal love. Of course, there *is* love between these souls, but not necessarily of the partnership kind in the current life. It can be very hard to accept this fact, and unrequited love is not a good basis for spiritual development.

However, twin souls, sometimes called twin flames, are another matter. If two souls are twinned in any one lifetime, they are definitely meant to be together.

My husband Tony and I are twin flames, and are destined to be partners in this life. I know this for several reasons. First, our relationship is of the kind that makes others comment in amazement on it. We don't argue, we always want to do what's best for the other one, and we never tire of each other's company. When you are in a relationship with a soul mate of this kind, they cannot annoy you, because they are so nearly a part of you that it would be like being annoyed with yourself.

Tony and I know of several lives where we have been together. The one that we feel was most influential was in the time when the legend of King Arthur came about, in the fifth to sixth centuries.

After having short flashes of memory, we decided to take a trip to South Cadbury, which is where we felt any real forts or castles having connections to the legends (which we believe were based in fact) would have been. South Cadbury is a huge earthen mound, with ramps around it. If you stand up there you can see Glastonbury Tor rising in the distance. The tor appears so unnatural from there, that it is easy to believe that the tales of the land in between once being under water are true. The only realistic explanation for the way the tor pokes up, all alone, is that it was once an island. Some legends say that the dead or dying "king" was taken to the tor by boat, and you can easily see how that might have happened.

We walked around the fort for some time and finally, by mutual consent, we chose an area to one side, to use for meditation/self-hypnosis. We lay on the ground and concentrated. Afterwards we compared notes and were astonished to discover that we had both experienced almost the same things while meditating.

We had both "seen" that we were gazing up at a wooden

roof, quite high, and could see thatching or straw between the beams. We had both noted flags and banners hanging on the walls, and concluded that this was a "great hall." We had both seen the door in the same place, and our descriptions of its construction matched perfectly. Tony had also seen something I didn't. I had heard a lot of crying and wailing, but hadn't seen who was doing it or why. Tony, on the other hand, had seen a crowd of people carrying a body aloft, over their heads.

Some time later we found out that excavations had indeed revealed the remains of a building, which it was believed was once the great hall of the fortress, in that very spot were we had our visions.

Tony and I made a contract before we came into this life that we would be together, and why. We both needed the support of each other in order to learn the lessons this life was to hold for us. We both understand what we are learning but, like most people, we sometimes have trouble understanding that there is an ultimate benevolent purpose behind every trauma we go through – for that is the way it is. It's hard to believe that sometimes, when we are stuck in our human form, but once you are past the bad times, and you look back, you can discern the map you have followed, and why it was necessary to follow it.

If you are lucky enough to find yourself with this kind of soul mate, it would be a huge mistake to take it for granted, or squander the opportunity. Your twin flame will, of course, always be a member of your soul clan, and this is comforting, because it means you will never lose each other.

CHAPTER 11

why we live more than once

Why We Live More Than Once

ONE LIFE IS NOT ENOUGH

How do we go about tying up loose ends, and why do we need to live more than once in order to do it? The answer is pretty obvious. If you accept any kind of life after death, and if you are in any way spiritually inclined, then you will easily see that one lifetime is never going to be enough to progress the soul.

There are all kinds of people in the world: mass murderers, child abusers, saints, kindly people, rich men, poor men, children who don't live beyond or even up to birth, nasty people, spiritual people, celebrities, oppressed people, privileged people, etc. The only thing that makes sense of all this is past lives. How else can all these souls have an equal chance at progression? There has to be a chance of every soul making it to a higher level, otherwise there is no point to this life, or to any other life after death. There has to be an equal chance for all, and in one lifetime that is just not going to happen. We have to experience all kinds of lives before we can start to understand what it means to have emotions, and use our responses to those emotions to grow.

The only way a spiritual being, which is what we are, can experience the whole gamut of emotions, is in the human form. When we are in spirit we see the whole of our being. We understand the whole of the cosmic plan and we know that the lives we live on this planet (or any other) are just a learning phase we go through.

This brings me to the subject of karma. Many people believe that this is a "what you sow so shall you reap" sort of thing. People write and ask me, "What did I do in a past life that makes me have such a bad one this time around?"

The answer to this is in two parts. First, we are not punished, for there is no judgement. When we pass into spirit, as I said, we have divine knowledge for that time. We can see where we came from, our progress and development, and where we are trying to get to. That being the case, we then choose, with the help of our Past Life Angel, the next set of experiences we need, either to learn more, or to enable us to understand a wrong that we perceive someone else has done to us. Our life might be selected as one of sacrifice, in order to assist another member of our soul clan. We might choose the next life to provide us with an opportunity to get right something we got wrong in a previous life, interacting with the same group of people we went through it with in the past.

Second, it is possible to block your human life by not remembering all this during it, so what can seem like bad luck can be your Past Life Angel trying to wake you up. Incidences that seem like a slap in the face can in reality be more of a slap in the subconscious. Unblocking your subconscious can also release the floodgates of the life you were meant to lead. Your subconscious is a kind of computer, and if you constantly feed negativity into it, it will do its best to make those negative things happen. This negativity can be caused by perceived guilt from a past life, even if you don't consciously remember it. This was part of my trouble, but once you see the past clearly, you can understand that guilt is not logical, because everything that happened is past, and that you are just the soul that evolved from that experience, you are not the person who caused it and is to blame for it. You can get over it and move on. This release can be a very good trigger into a better existence.

You can see how all this makes our Past Life Angels' jobs very difficult, and why we absolutely would never make it without their guidance.

Karma simply means "balance," and that is what we come here time and time again to achieve. This sometimes means that we have to experience a "bad" life. If every life was good and smooth and easy, it wouldn't achieve anything except in a transitory way.

Another question that I am often asked, along with the previous ones, is why there are more and more souls on this planet if they have all been here before. The answer to this is a matter of belief. I believe that there are many dimensions and also many other places where consciousness resides as well as on this Earth. I also believe that many of these souls are coming to the Earth at this time in order to make use of the massive learning opportunities there are in this place, in this age. Also, the fact that this planet is approaching the time of mass consciousness, and many souls want to experience that too.

HOW TO ACCESS PAST LIVES

One way is to be regressed is to go to a therapist. This involves a hypnotherapist taking you into a trance state. Put simply, this means that you become relaxed enough that your conscious mind, with all its associated noise and chaos, is quiet. The hypnotherapist will allow you to access that place of silence deep within. This will permit your subconscious mind, with a little encouragement, to come to the fore and reveal its hidden secrets. Every single life you've led, as well as every detail you've absorbed of your current lifetime, is stored in your subconscious. You will respond to the therapist's questions and thereby discover who you used to be.

There are several levels of depth of regression, and the after-effects and emotional involvement varies with the different platforms.

Level 1: This is not a very deep regression and you will only get glimpses of your past. As with most mediums' messages, the facts will be sketchy and you may well come out of the regression not quite sure if what you saw was real.

Level 2: In this level the picture will be very real. However, you will be viewing the events from a third party perspective, and the emotional involvement will only be a little stronger than if you were watching an emotive film. It will all seem very familiar to you, but you won't be quite sure if this was something that happened to you, or to someone else.

Level 3: At this level you will be aware of taking part in the events that unroll in front of you, and you may experience very empathic senses, such as taste and smell. The tale will seem a little surreal though, and may not be completely clear to you. There may be some confusion, and still you might feel as if the person taking part is not really you. This, as in the previous level, is because your body, mind, and soul are not yet quite reunited, and so that aspect of you which lived the life you are viewing, will still not feel quite like the real you.

Level 4: At this point all the emotions are very real, and will stay with you for the rest of your conscious lives. You will be very absorbed, and all the senses will be fully experienced. However, at this level you will still be peripherally aware of your current life and persona, and be aware that you are undergoing past life memories. The character in the events will be easily thought of as "I," but you will still answer the therapist's questions, using references to your current life, such as "I was older than I am now."

Level 5: This is as deep as you can get. You will be totally immersed in the past life, and have no awareness of your current life. You will answer questions in the present tense, such as, "I am walking down a narrow lane…" You will experience full detail and be aware of conversations, colors, and moods. It is at this level that caution with choosing your therapist is vital. When I went for my first regression, it was totally unexpected to the therapist that I went straight to this level. As a consequence of inexperience I was brought out very much still attached to that past life. Most people would need two or three sessions to reach this level. I don't believe I ever came fully back to the present, until I had a special healing session with Diane Egby Edwards.

The best way to find a therapist, if you can, is to go by personal recommendation. The caution is necessary because anyone can set themselves up as a regression therapist, even if they have never been trained in any way. The other thing that needs to be addressed is that a person can be a very experienced and competent hypnotist, and yet have very little or no experience of past life regression. You need to be with someone who has that knowledge, because the types of problems that can arise and need healing can be very different from the "normal." If someone you know has had a successful and life-shaping session with a therapist, then you can feel reasonably secure that you will too.

So, what do you do if there is no recommendation? You should ask your proposed therapist a few key questions.

How much experience have you had of past life regression in particular?

What safeguards will you put in, in case I am distressed by what I see?

How will you finish the regression and bring me out?

What will you do to heal my death in that lifetime?

What will you do to heal any traumas I remember?

What level will I reach?

The answers should be something along the lines of:

I have regressed many people, and have resolved their current life problems by exploring their past.

You will be able to come out of the session at any time if you want to. You'll be able to just ask me.

I will take you through your death in that life, so that the circle is completed.

I will bring you out to the light and let you look back and observe your body, so that you see that death is nothing to be feared.

I will talk you through the trauma and discuss with you what you learned from it. I will make sure that the trauma is released and stays in the past, where it belongs.

I will make sure that you only reach the levels gradually, and that if you progress to Level 5, I will bring you back slowly through the levels, to make sure that you are fully detached from the past.

Failure to do these things leaves you open to becoming "stuck" in that life, which has happened to me once. In my case, I believe it was necessary, but most people should avoid it.

SELF-HYPNOSIS

The other way to regress is by self-hypnosis. Contrary to what some people think, I believe this can actually be safer than a guided session. However, you might not get so many answers, dates, and facts, because no one will be asking you any questions. However, done this way, you will find out what you "need" to know. I think it's safer sometimes because your own Past Life Angel will be strictly in control, and I don't believe they would allow your subconscious to bring you into any harmful situations. Otherwise, with a therapist, you have to trust that they will have the ability and the will to let your angel take charge. This is why I devised and recorded my own Past Life Meditation CD, and I feel my experience can help others. At the very least this way will give you some clues to steer your therapist in the right direction. Therapy is expensive, and so if your subconscious has already targeted the relevant lifetime you need to see, it will save a lot of professional therapy time.

Nevertheless, therapy with a hypnotherapist may still be necessary. First, so that you can get answers to specific questions and, second, to help you if you are a person who finds it very difficult to "let go" enough to reach trance state.

DEPARTED SOULS

It's very important that any therapist, or self-hypnosis program, takes care of our natural apprehension about death. Of course, a belief in reincarnation itself is enough to make you understand that death is just a transition. There are, however, other areas when the emotional content of death-related experiences can make it hard to be logical about death, especially that of a loved one.

It's very hard when a loved one dies, and a lot of people become incapacitated for a long time, sometimes forever. Hard though it can be, this clinging to grief, and to the soul that's passed, is not the right thing to do for your spiritual progress. People sometimes ask me if past (and therefore future) lives are real, how is it that mediums can communicate and bring messages from people who have died, because surely those souls must have reincarnated and therefore be back on Earth? The answer to this is in several parts.

First, not everyone is ready, or needs, to come back to this planet. Some people come back here nine months after they died, and some come back up to hundreds of years later, or sometimes not at all. Therefore there are always a vast number of souls in spirit. They are often going through a time of healing, with their angel helping them, or discussing what they need to experience next, to learn, or to put right a wrong they did, and planning how that might happen. If they come back right away, it will be because they desperately need to interact again with someone they left behind on Earth. So, people who never hear from a deceased loved one again might consider that it could be because the loved one is back on the Earth, coming back into their lives, albeit as a different person.

Another reason that mediums can communicate with departed souls becomes obvious from the messages they bring. You first have to allow that mediumistic communication is not an exact science. Coming through is often difficult for the soul, and the medium often gets muffled contact, which means that the soul cannot be clear in their message. Because of this the message, apart from a few pieces of evidence to prove who they are, will be a very simple, "I'm OK. Don't worry about me. I'm happy." Obviously the soul cannot be too explicit, for instance saying "I'm going to be coming back – we all are," because they are not allowed to awaken people – the people have to do it for themselves. What the soul is trying to say is that they need to move on, but they are tied to their old persona, because there are loved ones on Earth who are suffering too much at their loss.

Compassionate souls cannot bear to move on to another life while their loved ones cannot move on with their life. So, there comes a point where we should all willingly let go of the grief that is tying our lost loves to their old life, so that they are free to stop watching over us and get on with their own progression.

While I am talking about departed souls, it brings me to another point.

GHOSTS

Some ghosts are part of someone's past life. Whereas some ghosts are nothing but "tape recordings," absorbed and then replayed by rocks and other materials, some are, in fact, who we were. When somebody dies unexpectedly, or traumatically, a trace of them gets left behind, and it's possible that in the next life, we can "collect" that trace. I had this experience for myself.

The house I had lived in as Madeleine Fitzgerald in the 1600s was reputed to be haunted. When I went to visit the house for the first time, I came away with more than confirmation of my memories. I also came away with a facet of my personality, which had been missing, restored. It was confidence and also the ability to say "no." This addition to my life was a large part of what allowed me to change it. The current owners have reported no signs of the ghost since my visit.

So, next time you hear of a haunting, question whether that ghost could be the remains of someone who is alive again today, and that the haunting would cease as soon as that part was collected by its owner. Also consider that if you listen to your Past Life Angel, and uncover who you were, maybe you too can gain some benefit to your personality.

CHAPTER 12

past lives and suicide

Past Lives and Suicide

J'd like to touch on the subject of suicide. Essentially, suicide is a form of fleeing the lessons that you have been sent, and therefore also fleeing your spiritual progress. The sad thing is that once we understand our lessons, the need for them diminishes and life can quickly get much better. I committed suicide back in the 1600s, and I am still "catching up" with the lessons I ran from at that time. As I understand each lesson, so it fades away and another takes its place. Each lesson becomes quicker to learn as I develop more, and life starts to take a clearer route with fewer hiccups.

While not everybody reaches a state low enough to end their life, I think most people would admit that although they appear alright on the outside, inside, like everyone else, they struggle to come to terms with life. This struggle being waged inside us as we try to understand why we are here and what it all means, is part of the human condition, but it is also another manifestation of our Past Life Angels trying to make us wake up. If there was no struggle then there would be no prize, and the prize of spiritual enlightenment is one worth fighting for.

In some cultures it is considered a sin to commit suicide, and some religions even go as far as to say that anyone who commits this "sin" is abandoned by God forever. This statement makes me quite angry. A person who makes this claim for their God seems to me to be a very confused person indeed. But of course these same people also believe there is only one life, so it must be a very cruel God who metes out eternal damnation after just one chance.

Why would any God go to the trouble of creating human souls and lives with all their complexities, and put us here on this Earth with just one chance to get it right, when our chances of doing that are so remote? It makes so much more sense that we are here to learn, in a schoolroom, sitting our "exams," and having to redo the year if we "fail." Of course there is no "fail" in the strictest sense of the word – failure is just another learning opportunity.

Of course suicide is not a good idea. It puts you back, means you still have to learn the same lessons in some later life, and causes extra lessons to be put into your "curriculum." But it is not a sin, like taking someone else's life, and people who have had a child leave them this way should not be subjected to the added torment of believing their child to be "damned for all eternity."

Another aspect of our development that needs to be taken into account when suicidal tendencies appear in us, is how much our actions are going to affect other people.

It's important that we discover a deep sense of responsibility and care, not only for ourselves but also for the rest of the conscious Universe. Anyone who leaves loved ones damaged by their own premature and emotionally violent departure alters the developmental process of other people, by changing the scenarios that were laid out for them. With a missing player, obviously the play cannot proceed as planned.

Diane Egby Edwards, the best regressionist I know, gives her thoughts on the matter of suicide:

We have been so conditioned to believe that suicide is a terrible crime, that God would punish us in some dreadful way. That imposed belief came about largely because the state/church would no longer have any control over us if we were willing to take our own lives. After all, would the pyramids have been built or the amazing works of art in Byzantium have been created if the slaves – the poor devils who did all the work – had thought for one minute that they could escape by taking their own lives, without risking the wrath of the gods? Suicide *had* to be a crime to keep control of the workforce!

However, suicide is not to be encouraged. Any set of circumstances in our lives we can *choose* to see either as unbearable tragedy or an amazing opportunity to grow in our understanding, our ability to love. We may be surprised to learn that, on a subconscious level, *we actually create the happenings in our lives to act as stepping stones toward greater understanding.*

The only dimension that needs to change is our ability to love. If we end our lives we have denied ourselves that opportunity to grow, and almost certainly we will create similar circumstances in another incarnation in order to give ourselves that opportunity again.

If a person is contemplating suicide, the very best thing he/she can do is to reach out for help, because there are many healers and helpers now who will gladly give their strength to help someone in need of it. There is no shame in asking for help – it is wiser to seek help than attempting to "go it alone."

If proof were needed that suicide does not condemn, then the story of Christian surely provides it. He was a young man who came to do Past Life Regression because he was "curious" about it. He had no idea that he had killed himself in an earlier lifetime. He remembered two past lives...

After the induction, now deep in hypnosis, he remembered a past life that was happy and fulfilling. Later he went to the memory of suicide in a subsequent lifetime.

"I'm wearing green baggy trousers, green hat and strap shoes... "

His name is John and he is on his way back to the town where he lives, having been out walking in the countryside. He's following the track, and there are sheep around him. As he approaches the town he notices the cobblestone streets, and a pub on the corner – it has a painted sign outside depicting a bearded man carrying an axe. There are houses with "small windows" and a lot of white. He goes over the bridge and now he's home. His pleasure at seeing his wife is apparent. She has auburn curls and big eyes. Her blue dress is corseted at the top and it billows in layers over her petticoat. Her name is Charlotte, and they are very happy together.

I guide him to a significant event in that life, which is the birth of a son. He is there, proud and happy, holding the baby, but is a little concerned for his wife, who is tired after the birth. There has been much blood.

Now we move on; it's some years later. They are in the same house. There's a big, wooden table in the kitchen. He can see his son has long fair hair; and now another baby boy has come into the family. John's going to do what he likes best – go walking in the countryside.

John now goes to the death in that lifetime. They live in a bigger house now. He's not as old as he'd like to be at his death. He finds himself lying in bed, his chest is painful. His son, now grown up, is beside him, "... wearing a waistcoat," John tells me with some pride. His wife, Charlotte, is so sad – she senses that he's about to die. He's coughing a lot and gently he moves into the death. It is over. He leaves his body and floats peacefully into the light. As he reviews his life he is content that it was a poor, but happy one.

The next lifetime he remembers is not so happy, though.

He is a jazz composer and musician. It's a lonely life. He seems to have little to do with his parents as, after a violent argument with his father one day, he is ordered out of the family home. His father doesn't like or approve of his music. Full of unhappiness, anger, and strong feelings of rejection he ends up living in a small flat in the city. Here he spends his days writing music and his nights playing double bass in a club. He is in France. He loves his music and is obviously good at it because a few years later he has become famous "... in a small way." There are few people in his life. He sometimes reads the newspapers and comments that "... there is a lot of unrest". The year is 1936.

One night after leaving the club, it's late and the streets are deserted. He is robbed. The thief holds a knife to him and he's very scared. His wallet is stolen, there's not much money in it, but afterwards he's very angry.

In the next scene he finds himself standing on a high bridge. Now in his mid forties, he's still very unhappy. He is estranged from his family and the few friends he has won't speak to him (he doesn't give the reason for the rift with his friends). Sad and confused he has decided to end it all.

"... I'm going to jump... I can't take any more." He throws himself into the water.

He drowns and as the pain ends feels "... much better now." I help him to do some healing on that lifetime before he finally leaves it, as there is still anger and bitterness. Focussing a beam of compassion and love energy onto the body he's just left, he uses this as a symbol for healing the whole lifetime. It can no longer have any negative effect in further incarnations. Now he floats into the light, it feels so good. There is a woman there to meet him; he's not sure who she is, but feels great love emanating from her.

And so that unhappy life is ended and all is well. Undoubtedly he will create again the opportunity for learning that those circumstances offered him, and next time he may "see it through" rather than end his life... or maybe not. Who knows? One thing is sure, though. He *will* get through it at some time – sooner or later.

I once committed suicide. In 1640 I followed what I thought was my husband, whom I knew to have been killed, through the house where we had lived. I followed him up the staircase and into the attic rooms. From there I looked out of the gable window and "saw" him below in the courtyard. I jumped.

This had many effects on me in this life. First, I have a fear of falling. We were recently on holiday and visited the Grand Canyon in America. I was fine while we had guard rails in front of us, but in many places there are sheer drops straight down, one mile to the bottom. The whole time we were near the edge I was worried that I, or indeed someone else, was going to fall off. I could feel the rush of air past my ears. I could feel my arms and legs turning, out of my control, and I could see the ground rushing up at me.

I think my fear (controlled now) of flying is also to do with this death in my distant past. It's not so much the flying as the possible falling that worries me. I am now able to control this fear, as I know where it comes from, and so it is for all past life induced phobias.

The other effect it had on me came later. It took me some while to pluck up the courage to re-experience my death in that lifetime. When I did (with the help of Diane Egby Edwards) I was very pleasantly surprised. There was no pain. When I hit the ground, there was just a burst of white light and, following Diane's instructions, I was able to look back at the body as it lay on the ground, and really understand that although my dead body was there, I, that inner part of me, was quite safe, quite whole, and able to look back dispassionately on the "envelope" I had inhabited for eighteen years.

I certainly would not entertain anyone blaming that poor girl for killing herself. She was out of her mind, and really I imagine her Past Life Angel knew that it had all been too much and there would be little to be gained by forcing her to continue her miserable existence. So, suicides are *not* damned for all eternity, not even for one second in fact. I do have to accept though that my act might have impeded the spiritual development of others I was interacting with at the time. I'm sure that the angels found a way to make it all come right for the others, but I know I must have caused at least a small problem.

The other effect the suicide had on me was, however, to make me realize that I needed to have more faith. That I should understand that you never lose anyone, and that all will be revealed when we are back in spirit.

CHAPTER 13

children and past lives

Children and Past Lives

Children are very much more open than adults when it comes to intuitive abilities, and in most cases they have past life memories, which they can relate if they are encouraged to do so.

It's surprising when you start asking, how many people know of, or have heard of, a child who has made strange statements, such as, "Where's my real Mummy?" or, "Before I was alive I had my own children." Or, of course, you get children who are obsessed with playing a certain game, who could be re-enacting a past life.

Children's "invisible friends" are often, in fact, memories of people they don't want to let go of, or even in some cases the child's Past Life Angel. There have been many incidences where children have taken their parents to a place and declared that it's the place where they once died. There are also many cases where a child spoke a language that they had not been taught. Here are two stories, which give evidence to the sad fact that children's spirituality is usually muffled as they grow up, or stifled as nonsense.

The first is of a little boy called Tom. Tom learned to speak, like most children, in a gradual manner. His baby babbling slowly started to sound like recognizable syllables. Like most babies, he started off with his own "pet names" for things, before he was able to pronounce the correct word. His parents didn't take much notice of the fact that he used words they had never heard of for wanting a drink and other things. They presumed it was just a baby thing that he would grow out of. Then one day a friend visited the house. After an hour or so, Tom woke up from his nap, and in his usual baby talk started asking for things. It wasn't long before the visitor asked in an amazed voice, "You do know that Tom is speaking perfect Greek don't you?"

Tom's parents might have treasured this, and encouraged the child to tell them where the language came from, but of course they just tried to forget that their son was in any way "weird," and set about training him to talk "properly." As time went on, Tom lost his ability to speak Greek and as he got older he also lost some other memories he had.

I always advise people that if their child does this, or makes statements that seem silly at the time, to try and tape them for a start. I also suggest that they gently question the child. For instance, about an "imaginary friend," ask the child what the friend's name is, where they come from, what they are wearing, etc. That way, the child will have a starting point to trace their past, when they are ready to do so.

The other story is the tale of a young man, who had a totally unknown child grasp him by the hand and pull him across to her mother, saying, "Mummy, this was my daddy when I was a little girl before." "Mum" of course was embarrassed, as was the young man at the time, and the child was "shushed," and told not to be silly.

These children seem to have had all notions of who they really are pushed out of them by the time they are six or seven.

Sadly, as children, we are generally steered away from "flights of fancy," whereas in fact these could more accurately be described as 'flights of reality"! In this way our soul gets separated from the mind and body and we don't really know who we are anymore, or what we came here to do. We have to get mind, body, and soul back together in order for our life to get back on track. This can be done by accessing past life memories. This helps our subconscious to remember who we really are and what we need to do. Once we understand this, we get the passion we need to achieve it, fulfillment from that achievement, and happiness from that fulfillment.

It happened to me as a child too. I was always cheerful, and a tomboy, enjoying messing around with horses and dogs and very happy-go-lucky. Little worried me, except that I was always abnormally compassionate. Couple this with a great sense of empathy, and it's easy to see why I spent most of my childhood years striving to make others happy. I can vividly recall what may have been the first time I got a nudge from my Past Life Angel. This incident might seem rather harsh but, as I said, these angels are not concerned with our physical lives, and will go to any lengths to wake us up.

I must have been about seven years old, and my dad was driving me to a nearby town. I was horrified when the car in front of us struck a small brown dog. The dog rolled along beneath the car, emerged in a tangle of legs from underneath it, and fell into the gutter in a senseless heap. The car that hit the dog stopped, but that wasn't anywhere near enough for me. I wanted my dad to stop so that I could try and help the dog. I begged and pleaded and cried for him to do so, but he wouldn't. I was told that it wasn't any of our business and that we didn't need to get involved. But I *was* involved.

That dog was part of me, like every other creature and person on the planet. At that very second I knew that for a certainty. Of course, this knowledge was smothered by the conventions of "minding your own business," and it wasn't until I was in my forties and fifties that I came to understand the knowledge I'd had as a seven-year-old.

This 'connectedness' with the Universe is a very vital part of our spiritual awakening. We have to come to understand that everything we say or do has a knock-on effect on the rest of humanity, the world, and ultimately the Universe. This is because everything in the Universe is composed of the same energy at a base level.

This realization, when it finally came to me, explained many other things. I'm often asked why some people can "see" and remember past life incidents that happened when they weren't actually there, back then at the time the event occurred. The answer also explains how mediums work, and that is by tuning in to the Quantum Universe. Recent discoveries in astrophysics have found that only 5% of the universe is visible. This means that 95% of the universe consists of dark matter and dark energy, which doesn't reflect light and the nature of which is therefore unknown. This obviously makes a complete nonsense of anyone stating that "such and such" does not exist, or is not possible. We have no idea what really exists around us or what is or is not possible.

Another "new" idea is that time is nonlinear; in other words it does not run in a straight line, from the past to the future. Instead it runs in parallel lines, which means that there is no past or future, only now. Mediums can train their minds to step across these time lines and therefore see into the past or the future. In the same way, your Past Life Angel can direct you to a time and place, and show you what might have happened that has relevance to you, in a past life, without you having ever been there in the physical at the time.

The experience I had with the dog at age seven wasn't enough to cause me to take the final leap, but it was a start, a building block. But at the age of fourteen something changed in me, society took me over, and I started to concentrate on material things.

My next nudge was when I developed an occasional abdominal pain, which worried me. Nevertheless I married at nineteen, and I was, and am still, blissfully in love with my husband. In later years my next nudge came as depression started to creep into my life, and the scary thing was that I could see no reason for it, and that also meant I could never find a cure. Things got worse when I started to have nightmares – more nudges. One of them involved my being raped. At first the nightmare only went that far, but it wasn't long before I dreamed that a man was hurrying to save me, and I began to wake up screaming the name

Ryan. This made no sense at all, as I didn't know anyone by that name.

The nightmares got worse, the depression got deeper, until eventually one day I was actually contemplating suicide as a way out. I couldn't see anything ahead of me but a slow downhill slide; it all seemed so pointless. It's clear to me now, in hindsight, that I was missing a huge part of myself, my spirit. The only thing stopping me from ending my life was the love of my husband and son. On the day in question, the day that saved my life, changed me out of all recognition, and brought my being back together, I was sitting alone.

I didn't realize it at the time, but my depression had finally reached the point where I could become open to a clear message for the first time. I can recall sitting, unable to move or think about anything, and as soon as I reached that point, I was open, my Past Life Angel grabbed the chance, and I heard a voice in my ear say very clearly, "Switch on the TV." I had no idea who was speaking inside my head, or why this message was telling me to do something as mundane as to switch on the TV, but, when you are as low as I was, you'll clutch at any straw, and so I obeyed. On the screen was the face of a man, and the picture juddered, seemingly stuck on this image, for a few seconds. I had no idea who the man was. There was a close-up of his eyes, and all I knew was that for some inexplicable reason the depression that had dogged me for years was gone, for good, and without a trace. This was the first change of many, and my first experience of how a past life memory can change your current life.

It was incredible and for a while I didn't try to explain it;

I just enjoyed it. I know now that the "voice" was actually my Past Life Angel speaking to me, and she was to guide my path in the future, for I suddenly discovered that I did have a future, and it was more amazing than I could have ever dreamed.

After a while I realized that the man on the TV bore a remarkable experience to the "Ryan" of my nightmares, although he was actually an American country singer called Garth Brooks. It didn't matter at the time, so long as I was better. Something else started at this time, which should have been creepy. A ghostly man's hand kept appearing, superimposed over mine, but it wasn't at all scary. I just felt comforted by this apparition. My second nudge from my Past Life Angel.

However, a couple of months later something even weirder and definitely frightening happened, as the waters of my past came tumbling out in a torrent that was so fast it almost washed me away. I was walking through the shopping center, in a dream world, hardly seeing what was in front of me. Then, as I passed a butcher's shop I felt compelled to look inside. The butcher was chopping a side of beef with a cleaver, and as the blade thudded into the flesh, the scene in front of me changed. I could see bright green grass, and the thud of the butcher's knife was matched by the thrust of a sword into a defenseless man who was lying on the grass. It was Ryan. I recognized him immediately. Blood spurted, contrasting horribly with the rich green. Ryan looked at me, mouthing the name "Madeleine." I reached out to him in his dying moments, and found myself back in the shopping mall, my hand against the glass. It was, of course, yet another nudge.

I felt sick, dizzy, disorientated, and I made my way along the shop fronts, leaning against the windows like a drunk. Either something very strange indeed was happening to me, or I was going completely mad. Either way I had to do something about it – but what? The abdominal pain I'd suffered got worse too, frighteningly so over the next few months. (Again I was getting force fed information. Whenever I switched off, messages came through.)

It was days later, when I was pouring out my story to a lady who used crystals, that she said the words that changed the whole picture. I had asked her how I could be dreaming of this man, and seeing visions of him when I had never even met him. She replied, "Not in this life maybe." (It's quite clear now that this lady was sent to me to bring this one clear message. I never saw her again).

I was shocked. A past life? Could it be? Could Garth Brooks be Ryan from the past? Eventually I went for past life regression. I was scared to go at first, having never contemplated anything of the sort. I tried to put it off, tried to find other ways, but it was unrelenting and insistent, until I finally knew that the only way to get peace was to find out the whole truth and accept it. During the session, the hypnotherapist became terrified, because my Past Life Angel took me over and out of her control. I had been steered and manipulated into the session, and the angel was going to make sure that I relived the right set of memories.

Tony, my husband, was downstairs in the therapist's house, alone. At one point he heard me crying hysterically and, worried, he was about to come to me. But, in his words, "The door behind me opened and someone came in. The being stood behind me and spoke in a language I couldn't understand, but the meaning was clear. I was told that everything was as it should be, and that I was to stay where I was. If someone had offered me a million pounds I could not have moved." It is very obvious to us today that Tony had a visit either from my Past Life Angel, or his.

After that session the memories flooded back to me: of my seventeenth-century life and, yes, Garth Brooks was Ryan, my husband, Ryan Fitzgerald.

Another interesting physical manifestation is that of scars. People who were stabbed or wounded to death in one area of their body will often bring through birthmarks or even unexplained scars to indicate that site. If they don't have something natural to mark the spot they will often create one, possibly in the form of a tattoo. One very strange thing I later discovered, to verify what I saw under regression, was that Garth Brooks has a scar in exactly the same place as where Ryan was stabbed. It seems that he has the scar while I had the pain. That pain disappeared, never to return, when I met Garth for the first time. This is another interesting phenomenon of past lives.

Since those moments I have become a successful songwriter, author, TV presenter of my own show on our local TV station, journalist, and feature writer. All of these things happened as a direct knock-on effect of my being woken up to my past. It was at about this point that my husband, Tony, and I were guided to up sticks and move from Norfolk to the county of Somerset. We literally packed up our belongings and left. At the time we had no idea why, but were just following the inner convictions that I felt.

This led us both to more past life memories, of a life we shared together, which I'll come to later. Neither of us has actually been able to recall any conversation where we decided to make this move. It must have been put in our minds while we were asleep. The more you listen, the more you hear, and the more you hear the more you listen, and so on.

Once we had settled near the town of Taunton, we started to wonder why exactly we were there. The area was very beautiful, but I was convinced that we had been guided there for a reason. Soon, because of my reputation as a local author, I was offered unpaid work as a columnist on the county newspaper. At the same time, various TV shows had become interested in my story and I was soon an old hand at appearing as a guest.

This is turn led me to apply for a job on the newly set up local TV station, and because of my experience I was accepted, and soon became the host of my own daily chat show. My guests were mostly mediums, clairvoyants, and people of that kind. The show ran for two years, right up to the dissolution of the station. It was during this time that I came to realize that there were so many people out there who were feeling the same as I was before my past caught up with me.

Later I started writing for magazines, and this was when I really began to understand how important it was for people to wake up to who they were, and get going in their lives on their real purpose for being here. Of course, not everyone is going to be led and instructed so dramatically by their Past Life Angel, but they will be led, if they are willing.

remembering your master plan and sticking to it

Remembering your Master Plan and Sticking to it

Your master plan is the ultimate goal for this lifetime and beyond. This is the plan you devised with your Past Life Angel and your soul clan before you came to this life. This scheme that you are meant to unravel and decipher can be almost anything you can think of, and probably a lot you can't. I'll give you a couple of examples. It can be something as simple as cutting a cord.

CORD CUTTING

Sometimes we bring through an overly strong connection to someone or something from a past life into our current one. If, for instance, we lost someone in a very traumatic or unfinished way, then there will still be a need to say goodbye properly before we can move on. The first thing to do is, of course, to discover if this is the case. Your Past Life Angel will be busy giving you clues, such as making sure you keep "coincidentally" seeing the person in this lifetime. Things can become quite difficult though, even with such a simple task. People can develop an obsession for the person that "mysteriously" seems to confront them, either physically or by image. This often manifests itself with someone who is famous because, of course, it's much easier to bring this person to your attention than it would be for your angel to show you someone unknown. This sort of thing only works well when your lifetime has coincided with the person you used to know being in the public eye this time, and therefore being highly visible. Unfortunately this brings with it a minefield of potential problems.

This is often how stalkers can be born. It's very easy to become confused, and the "fan" might think that they share a special bond with the celebrity. They may think that if only they could get close to the object of what they feel is their "affection," then the celebrity would see the truth, marry the "fan," and they would both life happily ever after. This is a special danger if the "fan" has no other loving partner, because they are then much more vulnerable to misconception. The truth is more straightforward, but can be harder to accept. The "fan" does have a special bond, but it's a bond that their angel is trying to show them needs to be cut. It's a carry-over from the past, not an invitation to the future.

If you find yourself in this situation, first have regression, to find out if and when you knew this person. Then it's fine to want to meet them, because that will aid in the cord cutting, but you must never expect anything back from the person, because their needs will most likely not be what you are hoping for. Their reaction will probably not be to welcome you with open arms, but to treat you exactly like any other fan, because they *have* moved on and are no longer tied to you.

What you must do is this: take yourself into a peaceful, relaxed state, and meditate if you are able. Then picture this person floating above you in a clear bubble. Picture them not as they look today, but how they looked back in the past when you knew them. Picture a silver cord running from the bubble to you. This cord does not represent the love that you shared – that can never be severed, and will be reciprocated and remembered when you are next both in spirit. All you are going to cut away is the pain associated with the loss of them, which, in this life, is a mere phantom. Imagine a pair of silver scissors in your hand, and, sending love and good wishes to the person, cut the cord.

Your immediate feeling may be one of greater loss but, after a while, the pain will ease, and you will find yourself able to observe the person from afar with a tranquil heart, and no longer feel the need to tread the edges of the dangerous waters of obsession. Bear in mind, also, that these inappropriate feelings you had may well have been holding you back in this life and be a barrier to you finding the soul you are meant to be with. If this task is the extent of your master plan this time, it may be that you have been stuck life after life, suffering unrequited love for this person. If this is the case, then your Past Life Angel will be able to get on with helping you attain the best you can in this life.

Your first goal here was to learn lessons, and this may well be the one you came here to learn. Some of these lessons can be bitter to swallow, but the good news is that once you have understood and have swallowed things will go more smoothly for you. When an uncomfortable lesson rears its head, try and step back and analyze just what you might be meant to learn from it. The quicker you can do that, the quicker the need for that lesson will fade away. Your master plan may simply have been to cut that cord, and you won't need to try and strike up a relationship with the person you knew in a past life.

Of course, there may be more that you are meant to achieve in this situation. Many people are here on the Earth this time for a specific reason, that of being a seed-planter. We are all cogs in the great cosmic machine, and we all have a part to play, big or small. When you uncover a past life, with a famous person or not, most times this is just something for you. Your angel has triggered it, just to aid your spiritual development. On the other hand, occasionally you are meant to dig for evidence of it. This evidence can then be used to open the eyes of other people in the world.

I'm putting in an example of how to cope with this in a way that will help you if you have been affected this way, because this kind of thing is very common, and sadly people suffering from this kind of ancient grief are often treated badly. Jewelle St James could never be accused of being a fan or stalker, because the person she knew in the past was killed in this life, before she understood her connection to him.

When John Lennon was brutally killed, the world stood still for a while, but for Jewelle St James the whole world came tumbling down. She was grief stricken, immobilized with regret for losing a chance to… what? She didn't know what her feelings meant, only that, devastatingly, it was too late. She didn't understand her feelings at all. She felt confused because she hadn't thought of John Lennon for over fifteen years, and yet all she could think of was that she should have paid more attention to him.

Her family life suffered as her grief overtook her. Try as she might to hide the pain, she felt like she was living a lie the whole time. She went about her wifely duties, pretending to be normal, while all the time she really just wanted to sit and cry all day. This went on for three long years. The world began to turn again for everyone else as they got over the shock of John's tragic death, while Jewelle wanted to scream at people, "Don't you care? John Lennon is dead!"

Finally, in a desperate attempt to find some answers, she went out and bought an album of his. While she was listening to the track, "Jealous Guy," she slipped into another time and place. She could see a narrow grassy lane and at the side there was an old granite milestone that read, "… miles to London." The number of miles was worn away and she couldn't read it. This was a typical Past Life Angel induced vision, but who could Jewelle tell, without being thought insane?

When she finally discussed it all with her mother, she told me that she had been attending a regular group in order to develop her psychic abilities, and she offered to try and tune in for Jewelle, to see if she could shed any light on what was going on. She did so, and told her daughter a remarkable story.

She said that in a previous life Jewelle had been a young lady called Katherine James, who had fallen in love with a man called John Baron. They had been betrothed in an English village near Castlemere, centuries ago, but John Baron had become ill and was taken away. He never returned and Katherine never had a chance to say goodbye to him. Jewelle's mother said she could hear the sound of chimes. She told her that John Baron was John Lennon. The cause, she said, of Jewelle's emotional destruction at his sudden and violent death was that she had known and lost John Lennon in a past life! She said that the song, "Jealous Guy," had been written by John about his past life as John Baron.

Jewelle was stunned, and talking to her husband made her realize how far-fetched it all sounded. She was determined to find out the truth one way or the other, so she planned to find Castlemere and go there, even though she would have to travel to England, from her home in Canada, to visit it. Much to everyone's surprise she did find the village of Castlemere. Well, at least she found the Castle of Mere, which she thought must be it, and flew to England. The whole visit was a total disaster. She had a lot of trouble getting to the village, as she hadn't reckoned with the lack of transport in that remote area. She only got to spend a single hour there and she couldn't find any records to back up her story. All that expense and time for nothing! For the first five days after she got home, she stayed in bed complaining of jet lag, but she was really suffering from a major let-down.

It was Jewelle's sister, Konni, who brought her back to life. Konni suffered from MS and, as the disease took hold of her, as a by-product it also released her psychic ability. She sent Jewelle a message to say that she *was* right, but had been looking in the wrong place. She told her sister that she should go to the village of Petworth to find her past. She told her that there was a hospital there, and that there was the sound of chimes where she had lived. Chimes... again.

Once she knew this, spontaneous memories started to come through thick and fast. She recalled her first meeting with John Baron and how he had graciously helped "Katherine" by giving her a ride in his cart to avoid the mud in the lane. She recalled working in a small hospital and nursing a dying man called Mr. Hatchett. She remembered going to her first dance and how a gallant John Baron and Katherine had danced. It was a joyous time, swaying around the dance floor in his arms.

It was bittersweet to remember all this but yet have no evidence to prove that she wasn't just daydreaming. Then she saw an advertisement for past life regression with a psychic called Laara Bracken. Excitedly, Jewelle made an appointment to see her.

The regression was a huge success. She remembered standing in what she described as a "golden" square in the 1680s, carrying a basket of bread. She also remembered more details of Katherine and John and their time together. She recalled her despair when he was taken ill and her desperation to find him after he was taken away to die. When she came round, her cheeks were wet, but her head was crystal clear. She had to go to Petworth. To go home.

So she made her second journey to England and this time it was quite different. She found "Golden Square" in the village, the old bakery building that still stands; she found the old hospital and the records of Katherine James and John Baron, and she even found records for Mr. Hatchett. She walked around the village, crying at every turn, as she recognized more and more features – everything was as she'd seen. The chimes turned out to be from a water clock that rang every hour from the town's market square, and the milestone, though since removed after being hit by a lorry, had once stood at the side of the lane, announcing "49 miles to London." Probably the most astounding thing that happened was that she found herself, chillingly, staying in the very same attic room where Katherine James had died!

So, she had no doubt that she had been Katherine, but was John Lennon also John Baron? Jewelle consulted with many psychics about this. She always knew when one was genuine because John's code word was "dance." If the medium knew that without her saying a word, then she knew they were genuine. One told her that John Lennon had confirmed that my story was true and that he wanted her to know that Emily Brontë was his favorite writer.

Some time later she had a message from another genuine psychic. John told her, "The answer is to accept what the spirit has informed you is correct. Your lives were as stated, don't question the facts. John and Katherine, the music, the dancing, all belong to that life together…" He also told her that in another past life he had been Branwell Brontë. So, the psychics, without knowing each other, had all confirmed what Jewelle knew to be true.

Other messages came later. "I am in a very enlightened place. I am in a circle of energy, a pure crystalline light, a beautiful place. I have so many masters; we in spirit can affect change on earth and will affect change." "Trust and believe in love. Love is really all there is, that is, all there is, is love." One of Jewelle's most precious messages from John was, "The dancing hasn't stopped. Still dancing with you, just a different place."

This story of Jewelle St James not only demonstrates

beautifully how easily a Past Life Angel can communicate with you once you open the floodgates to it, but how validation can come in many different ways – through psychics as well as regression. Past Life Angels will often send messages through psychics, but having a "code word" the way she did helped Jewelle sort out who was genuinely in contact with her angel. Jewelle was able to go ahead and cut the cord that ensnared her to the past, and no longer feels a need to go on a "pilgrimage" to the place where she used to live as Katherine.

Another master plan that's quite common is that of unfinished business.

UNFINISHED BUSINESS

If you are the type of person who, in this life, just can't relax until all the "Ts" have been crossed and the "Is" dotted, then your angel may well be telling you that you have "unfinished business" from a past life. This business may well involve another person or, literally, business, or it could just be that you died just before you could complete some ambition or other.

Again, the first move is to discover, by regression, what the thing is that needs "finishing." Once you put yourself in the hands of a competent therapist (or use an appropriate method of self-hypnosis, such as my Past Life Meditation CD), you can be sure that your delighted angel will make sure you are guided to the right past life, the one that needs sorting out. There may, of course, be others, with other issues, but the one you go to will be the priority.

An example would be one such as that of Graham, who was born a Virgo, which was no coincidence either. Your birth sign is often another nudge in the direction you should be going. Graham always wanted things just "so," and could get very uncomfortable when they were otherwise. His Past Life Angel was feeding him these niggles and moments of discontent in order to trigger his memories.

Eventually, as is often the case, when he was ready, Graham met someone who was a believer in past lives, and who guided him to be regressed. Once this was done he discovered that he had made a promise, centuries before, that he had been unable to keep. He was able to rediscover the person he had made the promise to, and help them in a way completely unrelated to the previous promise, but nevertheless in a satisfying way. This task accomplished, he was able to progress both spiritually and materially in his life.

Your master plan may, of course, be of global proportions. When you look around the world today you can see people who are apparently passionately driven by something so strong that it makes them appear able to withstand things that would turn most of us insane with anger and frustration. Take, for instance, Nelson Mandela, who was imprisoned unjustly for a large portion of his life, and yet on release has worked so tirelessly on behalf of other people that he has been awarded the Nobel Peace Prize. Most people, surely, would have been bitter and spent the rest of their lives seeking revenge or compensation for what happened to them. It is clear that people such as this are following their master plan, and this gives them such joy and satisfaction that all else matters not at all. He does not grieve for his lost life, because he knows he has achieved what he came here for.

Another such person would be the Dalai Lama, who in 1959 was forcibly exiled from his homeland of Tibet by the Chinese government. This was punishment for his efforts to bring about a peaceful solution to Sino-Tibetan conflict. And yet, far from showing bitterness, the Dalai Lama has dedicated his life to equanimity and teaching tolerance and good humor. It is obvious that he too is fulfilling his master plan, and is content because of it.

CHANGING THE WORLD FOR ONE PERSON

Of course, not everyone's plan involves changing the world. There are those who came here not to be the one man who changed the whole world, but to be the man, or woman, who changed the world for one person. The signs of this from your angel might be constant little lessons and messages that love is the most important lesson of all. To selflessly love one person, to the extent that you remake their world around them, is often the master plan.

Some people can be quick to criticize the "little housewife" who has no ambition but to make a home, who feels no discontent with living for someone else, perhaps her children or husband. But perhaps in a past life this person learnt the hard way to avoid at all cost neglecting your children or loved one, and has made a contract this time around to compensate them for something that transpired in the distant past.

So, assuming that by now you are getting the idea and your only problem is that you feel unfulfilled, how do you remember and implement your master plan and stick to it? The way is to become like a sheep. You need to allow yourself to be led.

Everybody will empathize with the saying, "banging your head against a brick wall." Well if you find yourself doing this, then you have to learn to accept, quietly and calmly, that you are going the wrong way, trying to proceed in the wrong direction, and *not* following your master plan.

You will soon start to realize that in fact you don't need to know the whole extent of your master plan. If you knew everything, you might try to pre-empt it and in doing so ruin the flow of things. If you look and listen and take note when you are being told, "No, this is not the right way for you," and move ahead in the direction that has been smoothed for you, you will soon be looking back across time and seeing exactly how your angel's plan all came together, to bring you to where you are. That is not to say that you won't sometimes have to struggle, but if you keep faith you will soon see a way ahead and that will be the right way.

As you tune in more and more to your angel, and your subconscious, which contains all the knowledge you accrued from this and every other life you've had, you will start to feel intuitively which direction you should go in. Once you take a tentative step in that direction you will soon have your feelings validated if they are right, because doors will open and you will get the feeling that you are being "invited" to continue.

Your map through life has been carefully plotted for you and by you, so it should be relatively smooth, although you will continue to come up against lessons now and again all through your life. You will also come up against the occasional annoyance, but always try and see the energetic reasons there might be behind them.

Walk in your truth, stand tall in your light, and know that you are a wondrous being, the extent of which you can only imagine while you are in human form. You are here for a purpose that is vital both for the progression of your soul and the fate of every person on the planet. The signs are there, and you just have to open your eyes. The messages can be heard, and you just have to listen. So, be like that sheep and relax. Let your Past Life Angel lead you and accept that a setback is not what it seems. Setbacks are just nudges in the right direction and, just like a parent guiding a child who is learning to walk back onto the straight path, your angel will help you stay on track.

Can your master plan change? Yes it can. Some therapists are now able to "progress," as opposed to "regress," patients. This means that they are able to take their patients to see what their future lives will bring. I suppose in this case Past Life Angels become "Future Life Angels." I feel that this is an area to be careful about, because a little knowledge of the future can be a dangerous thing, as the future is not set in stone. However, in some instances, especially if your angels are sending visions of some future time, it is something that should be done. It's a very interesting exercise if future lives are accessed before and after past life healing, and recognition, has taken place, to see the difference. Obviously, if unfinished business, etc. gets resolved, the future life will change, and of course so will the master plan for that life. It would be a great help with people who are suffering from "carousel syndrome," because they would be able to see how much better their next life would be if they broke the cycle. ❖

I'd like to add a final word on happiness. This is what everyone is seeking. Some look for it in material possessions, some in competitive sport, some in relationships, and some in a bottle, but all of these things are fleeting. The way to happiness lies through passion. Passion does occur in the things I've listed too, but it fades, either through familiarity or age and loss of ability or, in the case of drink or drugs, with the permanent numbing of the emotional mind.

This is why I get letters from people who even though they are with someone they love very much, still feel depressed and still feel as if something is missing from their lives. This is why I was depressed, despite being with Tony who means more to me than I do to myself. Both I, and the people who write to me, feel bad because deep inside they know that someone else cannot make them whole. No matter how much being with that person means to them, they know they can only become whole by, and with, themselves. This applies to the people who feel that there is a deep hole inside them that nobody can fill, because they are right, nobody can fill it, because nobody else has the right stuff. It can only be filled by the person themselves and the substance to fill that hole resides in their distant past. This is what Past Life Angels are trying to tell us.

Love is the most vital and the most wonderful emotion we are capable of, and as such it is essential to our spiritual progress. It is required for any soul to be able to advance, and the ability to love advances any soul. But some people spend their whole lives waiting for and looking for a soul mate to fall in love with, and this can be almost as much of a waste of the soul's life as hankering after other "holy grails" of happiness, such as wealth and fame. Love is the best thing we as humans can achieve, but it does not automatically bring fulfillment to that soul. If your master plan was to come to the earth to love and be loved, then that *is* your 'holy grail', but if your purpose was something else, you can miss it by spending all your energy trying to attain something you were never meant to.

Enduring passion needs progress to sustain it, and once you are on your right life path, you will experience a passion like no other. Because your path moves constantly forwards, so will your passion. It is this emotion that brings you joy with every tiny step forward along your path. It is eternal and will never die, anymore than your soul will.

therapists

UK

Steve Burgess – Hull
Tel: 01482 326408
Email: steve@naturaltherapy.karoo.co.uk
Web: www.steveburgesshypnosis.com

Jill McCafferty – Taunton
Tel: 01823 276528
Email: jillmac@tiscali.co.uk

Barrie Anson – Chard
Tel: 01460 63238
Email: barrieanson@tiscali.co.uk
Web: www.alternativehealing.co.uk

Richard Murphy – Taunton
Tel: 01823 421101

Douglas Craddock – Manchester
Tel: (0161) 282 9291 / 0161 881 7171.
Email: hypnosis@karma7.supanet.com

Jeanette Sitton – London
Riverside Private School of Complementary Therapies, London
Tel: 020 8376 8088
Email: info@riverside-workshops.co.uk
Web: www.jsitton.pwp.blueyonder.co.uk/riverside/therapy.htm

Kim Thomas – Past Life Healing Courses Internationally
Tel: 01206 521177
Email: kim@angelshealing.com
Web: www.angelshealing.com

Anne Sylvester – York
Tel: 07734 245638
Email: info@hypnoandreiki.com
Web: www.hypnoandreiki.com

Effie Gardner – Leeds
Tel: 0113 261 2658
Email: info@effie-gardner.co.uk

Diane Egby Edwards – Bournemouth
Tel: 01202 423111
Email: Hypnotherapyworks@btopenworld.com
Web: www.hypnotherapyworks.org

Dave Goodfellow – Yorkshire
Tel: 01423 322325
Email: dave.goodfellow@btinternet.com
Web: www.hypno-therapists.co.uk

Brenda White – Newark
Tel: 01636 677725
Email: bwhite@uk-therapists.net
Web: www.bwhite.uk-therapists.net/past_life_therapy.htm

Sonia Desiderio – London
Tel: 020 8969 8966

Mano Warren – Glastonbury
Tel: 01458 833114

Julie-Anne Taylor – Edinburgh
Tel: 0131 478 2767/ 07771 605234

Margaret Lewis-Powlette – Bedford
Tel: 01234 327090 / Mobile: 07834733010
Email: Spiritess04@aol.com

Julie Winstanley – Warrington
Tel: 01925 422939
Email: julie@therapy4all.com
Web: www.pastlifetimes.com and www.therapy4all.com

Nicholas Crocker – Tintagel
Tel: 01840 770049

Judith Stone – Dronfield
Tel: 01246 419038
Email: jude.stone@btopenworld.com

Louise Hutchings – Newquay (Wales)
Tel: 0845 2269 345
Email: info@hypnotherapy-success.co.uk
Web: www.hypnotherapy-success.co.uk/

Julie Gale – Andover
Tel: 01264 393361
Email: juliegalehypno@aol.com

Carolyn Maybray – Broughton Astley
Email: carolyn.maybray@ukonline.co.uk
Web: www.pastliferegression-uk.com

Eileen Blacklock – Staines
Tel: 01784 459653
Email: eileen.blacklock@btinternet.com

Nicola Dexter – Camden/Edgeware
Tel: 020 7267 4706 / 020 8201 0604
Email: hypno@nicoladexter.com
Web: www.nicoladexter.com

Caroline Byard – King's Lynn
Tel: 01328 730256 / Mobile: 07919 525530
Email: carrieq@freenet.co.uk

Nikki Durrant – Billingshurst
Tel: 01403 780945
Email: nikkidurrant@hotmail.com
Web: www.nikkidurrant.com

Louise Hutchings – Jersey

Tel: 0845 2269 345

Email: info@hypnotherapy-success.co.uk

Web: www.hypnotherapy-success.co.uk

Dr. Rita C. Fichera – London

Tel: (020) 8800 0265

Email: fenice@ukonline.co.uk

Web: www.thephoenixpractice.co.uk

Janet Thompson – East Sussex

Tel: 01273 207 393

Email: mailme@janetthompson.org

Web: www.JanetThompson.org.uk

Andrew Hillsdon – Devon

Tel: 01409 211559

Email: info@pastliferegression.co.uk

Web: www.pastliferegression.co.uk

Tania Cheslaw – Cambridge

Email: tanche_therapy@yahoo.co.uk

Web: www.taniacheslaw.co.uk

Dr. Christine Elvin – Northampton

Tel: 01604 768343

Email: Christina@oesassociates.co.uk

Web: www.oesassociates.co.uk and www.create-the-reality.com

Reiko Rela Iwano – St Johns Wood

Tel: 020 7624 5495

Email: rela@iwano.plus.com

Web: www.violethillstudios.com/reikoiwano

Dave Laing – Liverpool

Tel: 0151 931 4391

Email: hypno@davelaing.co.uk

Web: www.davelaing.co.uk/hypno

Simon Childs – Aberaeron, Emlyn and Carmarthen, Wales

Tel: 01545 570812

Practice: 0870 242 0545

Email: hypno-plr@yahoo.co.uk

Dr. Sun Li – Edinburgh

Tel: 0131 666 0929

Stan Gerard – Scotland

Tel: 01224 213 808 / Mobile: 07730 468 183

Email: stan.gerard@whsmithnet.co.uk

Web: users.whsmithnet.co.uk/stan.gerard

HOLLAND

Anita Groenendijk – Wageningen

Tel: (0317) 425251

Email: a.groenendijk@chello.nl

Web: members.ams.chello.nl/a.groenendijk/english.htm

Hans TenDam – Ommen

Tel: 031-523-649949

Email: hwtendam@tasso.nl

Web: www.tasso.nl

EQUADOR

Mehra Atul Kumar

Tel: 593 9 733 940

MALAYSIA

Suesi Chong

Tel: 012-2808301

Email: suesie@treeofliferemedies.com

Vivienne Leong

Tel: 6019 3317 452

SOUTH AFRICA

Kim Morris

Tel: +2711826538419

Email: kim@soulconnection.co.za

Web: http://www.soulconnection.co.za

Jacques Theron – Cape Town

Tel: 0027 21 439 5041 / Mobile: 0027 82 817 5266

Email: inspire@telkomsa.net

Web: www.inspire-network.com

SPAIN

Maria Gemma Saenz (author of *Bases y metodologia de la TRCD*)

Tel: 0034 93 2800016

Email: info@openliferevista.com

Web: www.openliferevista.com

AUSTRALIA

Rosemary Wade – New South Wales

Tel: 02 6676 0874

Email: rosemarylifemagic@dodo.com.au

Sandy Hounsell – Queensland 4214

Tel: 61 7 5574 4256

Email: healingfromwithin@bigpond.com

Web: www.soul.awaken.com

Darrell Suckling NPM, IRPH – Queensland 4210

Tel: 07 5571 1505

Email: hypno@primus.com.au

Web: www.oe-pages.com/EDUCATION/College1/hypno

Dr. Frank Jockel PhD – Victoria

Tel: +61-3-9885-0440

Email: frank@thefutureis.com

Web: www.thefutureis.com

GERMANY

Davor Antunovic

Tel: 7153/72621

Email: davor.antunovic@t-online.de

Ulf Parczyk

Tel: ++49 (0) 61 09 / 50 84 30

Email: info@esopsych.de

Web: www.esopsych.de

USA

Jean Conway – Blue Moon Healing Center – MA

Tel: 001 413 774 7171

Web: www.hypnosiscenter.com/hypnotherapist-directory/jean-conway.htm and

www.bluemoonhealingcenter.com/index.html

Lauren Swanberg – WA

Tel: day (253) 572-2909

Tel: eve (253) 884-9179

Email: tiare01@msn.com

Dr. Robert Guffey – Texas

Tel: 903395-0465

Email: sevenplanes@sevenplanes.org

Web: www.sevenplanes.org/cd.htm

Dawn Marie Lannon – New York

Tel: day (914) 261-4784

Tel: night (914) 965-1996

Email: dawnlannon@aol.com

Karen Sullivan – IL

Tel: 847-717-3290

Email: karensullivan@wideopenwest.com

Web: www.dreamstudy.com

Carol Lovato – OK

Tel: 580-614-1473

Email: desperados@pldi.net

Roger Literski – MO

Tel: 314-731-4515

Email: northcountyhypnosiscenter@hotmail.com

Sunny Satin – California

Tel: (949) 689-4513

Email: californiahypnosis@yahoo.com

Web: www.lifefirst.com/ssatin

Laurie Greenberg – New York

Tel: (212) 501-3707

Email: DrLGreenberg@aol.com

Web:

www.soulcenteredtherapy.com/textfiles/pastliferegression.htm

Katie Kane – Kentucky
Tel: 770-975-8190
Email: katie_kane@hotmail.com
Web: www.prosperity.com/kane

INDIA
Sunny Satin – New Delhi
Tel: (0124) 235-7411.
Email: californiahypnosis@yahoo.com
Web: www.lifefirst.com/ssatin

SWITZERLAND
Bruno Meier
Tel: 0041-62-8781458
Email: reinkarnation@bluewin.ch

Other therapists in Switzerland can be found here:
www.gesund.ch/index.html?info?/verzmeth/reinkarn.htm

ISRAEL
Georgina Johnson
Tel: 972 4 9541953 or 972 050 6769464
Email: harans@netvision.net.il
Web: www.geocities.com/veratherapy

RUSSIA
Pavel S. Gyngazov
Tel: + (73822) 512850
Email: 4749@mail.tomsknet.ru

CANADA

Thelma Beam

Tel: 416 924-7215

Email: ccr@pathcom.com

Web: www.MindMeldConsulting.com

Dr. Georgina Cannon – Ontario

Tel: (416) 489-0333 / Toll Free: (866) 497-7469

Email: info@ont-hypnosis-centre.com

Web: www.ont-hypnosis-centre.com/contact/contact.htm

PHILIPPINES

Beatrice Seligbon

Mobile: 09204883749

Email: bethseligbon@digitelone.com

Web: www.col.com./seligbon and

www.iarrt.org/members/philippines/seligbon.html

BRAZIL

Herminia Godoy (author of *Terapia da da Regressão*)

Tel/Fax: 55-5740510

Email: cdhpg@osite.com.br

Web: www.centrodedifusao.cjb.net

GREECE

Carolyn Clark

Tel: (+30) 210 6253882.

Email: carolyn@karmafix.com

Web: www.earth-network.org

O

is a symbol of the world,
of oneness and unity. O Books
explores the many paths of wholeness
and spiritual understanding which
different traditions have developed down
the ages. It aims to bring this knowledge
in accessible form, to a general readership,
providing practical spirituality to today's seekers.

For the full list of over 200 titles covering:

- CHILDREN'S PRAYER, NOVELTY AND GIFT BOOKS
- CHILDREN'S CHRISTIAN AND SPIRITUALITY
- CHRISTMAS AND EASTER
- RELIGION/PHILOSOPHY
- SCHOOL TITLES
- ANGELS/CHANNELLING
- HEALING/MEDITATION
- SELF-HELP/RELATIONSHIPS
- ASTROLOGY/NUMEROLOGY
- SPIRITUAL ENQUIRY
- CHRISTIANITY, EVANGELICAL
  AND LIBERAL/RADICAL
- CURRENT AFFAIRS
- HISTORY/BIOGRAPHY
- INSPIRATIONAL/DEVOTIONAL
- WORLD RELIGIONS/INTERFAITH
- BIOGRAPHY AND FICTION
- BIBLE AND REFERENCE
- SCIENCE/PSYCHOLOGY

Please visit our website,
www.O-books.net

Some recent O Books

REIKI MASTERY
For Second Degree Students and Masters
David Vennells

Reiki has many levels and forms, and has changed along the way from the pure, "original" practice of its Buddhist founder, Dr. Mikao Usui. Advanced Reiki, especially above First Degree, is about "facing the mirror," the inner mirror of our own mind. As we progress with our spiritual practice we can begin to clean away the layers of misconception that colour the way we view ourselves, others and the world around us. This is a compassionate, wise, handbook to making the most of the Life Force Energy that surrounds and informs us all.

David Vennells is a Buddhist teacher of Reiki and the author of *Reiki for Beginners*, *Bach Flower Remedies for Beginners*, *Reflexology for Beginners*.

1-903816-70-X
£9.99 $14.95

LET THE STANDING STONES SPEAK
Messages from the Archangels revealed
Natasha Hoffman with Hamilton Hill

The messages encoded in the standing stones of Carnac in Brittany, France, combine and transcend spiritual truths from many disciplines and traditions, even though their builders lived thousands of years before Buddha, Christ and MuhammAd. The revelations received by the authors as they read the stones make up a New Age Bible for today.

"an evergreen..a permanent point of reference for the serious seeker."
Ian Graham, author of *God is Never Late*

Natasha Hoffman is a practising artist, healer and intuitive, and lives with her partner Hamilton in Rouziers, France.

1-903816-79-3
£9.99 $14.95

TORN CLOUDS
Judy Hall

Drawing on thirty years experience as a regression therapist and her own memories and experiences in Egypt, ancient and modern, *Torn Clouds* is a remarkable first novel by an internationally-acclaimed MBS author, one of Britain's leading experts on reincarnation. It features time-traveller Megan McKennar, whose past life memories thrust themselves into the present day as she traces a love affair that transcends time. Haunted by her dreams, she is driven by forces she cannot understand to take a trip to Egypt in a quest to understand the cause of her unhappy current life circumstances. Once there, swooning into a previous existence in Pharaonic Egypt, she lives again as Meck'an'ar, priestess of the Goddess Sekhmet, the fearful lion headed deity who was simultaneously the Goddess of Terror, Magic and Healing.

Caught up in the dark historical secrets of Egypt, Megan is forced to fight for her soul. She succeeds in breaking the curse that had been cast upon her in two incarnations.

Judy Hall is a modern seer who manages the difficult task of evoking the present world, plus the realm of Ancient Egypt, and making them seem real. There is an energy behind the prose, and a power in her imagery which hints that this is more than just a story of character and plot, but an outpouring from another age, a genuine glimpse into beyond-time Mysteries which affect us all today. Alan Richardson, author of *Inner Guide to Egypt.*

Judy Hall has been a karmic counsellor for thirty years. Her books have been translated into over fourteen languages.
1 903816 80 7
£9.99/$14.95

IS THERE AN AFTERLIFE?

David Fontana

The question whether or not we survive physical death has occupied the minds of men and women since the dawn of recorded history. The spiritual traditions of both West and East have taught that death is not the end, but modern science generally dismisses such teachings.

The fruit of a lifetime's research and experience by a world expert in the field, *Is There An Afterlife?* presents the most complete survey to date of the evidence, both historical and contemporary, for survival of physical death. It looks at the question of what survives-personality, memory, emotions and body image-in particular exploring the question of consciousness as primary to and not dependent on matter in the light of recent brain research and quantum physics. It discusses the possible nature of the afterlife, the common threads in Western and Eastern traditions, the common features of "many levels," group souls and reincarnation.

As well a providing the broadest overview of the question, giving due weight to the claims both of science and religion, *Is There An Afterlife?* brings it into personal perspective. It asks how we should live in this life as if death is not the end, and suggests how we should change our behaviour accordingly.

David Fontana is a Fellow of the British Psychological Society (BPS), Founder Chair of the BPS Transpersonal Psychology Section, Past President and current Vice President of the Society for Psychical Research, and Chair of the SPR Survival Research Committee. He is Distinguished Visiting Fellow at Cardiff University, and Professor of Transpersonal Psychology at Liverpool John Moores University. His many books on spiritual themes have been translated into 25 languages.

1 903816 90 4
£11.99/$16.95

THE QUEST

Joycelin Dawes

What is your sense of soul? Although we may each understand the word differently, we treasure a sense of who we are, what it is to be alive and awareness of an inner experience and connection with "something more." In *The Quest* you explore this sense of soul through a regular practice based on skills of spiritual reflection and be reviewing the story of your life journey, your encounter with spiritual experience and your efforts to live in a sacred way.

Here you become the teller and explorer of your own story. You can find your own answers. You can deepen your spiritual life through the wisdom and insight of the world's religious traditions. You can revisit the building blocks of your beliefs and face the changes in your life. You can look more deeply at wholeness and connection and make your contribution to finding a new and better way.
So well written, constructed and presented, by a small independent group of individuals with many years experience in personal and spiritual growth, education and community, that it is a joy to work with. It is a life-long companion on the spiritual path and an outstanding achievement; it is a labour of love, created with love to bring more love into our world. Susanna Michaelis, *Caduceus*

1 903816 93 9
£9.99/$16.95

THE LETTERS OF PAUL

Sylvia Moss

Paul's letters as they were meant to be understood

The letters of Paul are among the foundation documents of Christianity and of Western civilisation. But they were written by a man of a very different time and culture to our own. Cosmopolitan and educated as Paul was, his attitudes were circumscribed by the beliefs of the time. But his spirit is still with us.

If you believe that nothing survives death, or that there is no contact between those that have passed on and us here today, then this book is not for you. But if you accept that there are higher realms of consciousness, that can at times communicate with us, then this book is revelation. Years ago Lewis Durham, former pastor of the Glyde Memorial Church in San Francisco, asked what service he could give to the world. The answer was channelled through his friend Sylvia Moss; the revising of the letters of Paul by the one who was incarnate as Paul. This is what Paul would write today.

Sylvia Moss was closely connected for many years with the Findhorn Community in Scotland, and then founded the Alcyone Centre, a retreat centre for spiritual and environmental education, in Southern Oregon, where she lived for many years.

1 903816 94 7
£14.99/$19.95

THE JAPANESE ART OF REIKI
Bronwen and Frans Steine

Reiki techniques originated in Japan, in an intensely spiritual period of that country's history. This fully-illustrated book traces the system's evolution from a spiritual self-development system to a direct hands-on practice. The journey moves from Japan to the USA, out to the world, and back to Japan.
Focussing on the basic elements in their historical context, this guide contains beautifully grounded information that captures a unique sense of the system's traditional Japanese roots. The clarity and accessibility of the teachings in the book redefine and strengthen the concept of Reiki as it is practised today.

Reiki Masters *Bronwen* and *Frans Steine* are the founders of the International House of Reiki. They have worked with Reiki and researched it for many years, their particular passion being the recovery of traditional Japanese Reiki. They live in Sydney, Australia.

1 90547 02 9
£12.99/$19.95